About the Author

Ansu Kamara was born in a village in Sierra Leone, West Africa, to loving parents and had a childhood full of adventure and opportunity. As a young man, he made his way to America on a prayer and a student visa, determined to build a brand new life in the country of his dreams. He worked for decades in the printing industry, rising into managerial and leadership positions at several prominent companies. He is now living in San Antonio, Texas, with his wonderful wife, Evelyn. They have three children and preserving his life's story for them was a driving force behind this book's creation.

Dedication

I would like to dedicate this book to my older brother, Abu Bakarr Kamara, and to all the people of Sierra Leone and the world who have suffered from smallpox.

Ansu Kamara

DRIVEN BY HOPE

One Man's Incredible Journey to America

AUSTIN MACAULEY PUBLISHERS™

LONDON ✦ CAMBRIDGE ✦ NEW YORK ✦ SHARJAH

Ordering Information:
Quantity sales: special discounts are available on quantity purchases by corporations, associations, and others. For details, contact the publisher at the address below.

Publisher's Cataloging-in-Publication data
Kamara, Ansu
Driven by Hope: One Man's Incredible Journey to America

ISBN 9781641829113 (Paperback)
ISBN 9781641829120 (Hardback)
ISBN 9781645366409 (Epub e-book)

Library of congress Control number: 2019939280

The main category of the book — Biography & Autobiography / Personal Memoirs

www.austinmacauley.com/us

First Published (2019)
Austin Macauley Publishers LLC
40 Wall Street, 28th Floor
New York, NY 10005
USA

mail-usa@austinmacauley.com
+1 (646) 5125767

Acknowledgments

I am forever grateful to the outstanding team at Graphic Fine Color who recognized my hard work with the following honors over the years:

- 'The Safety Man of the Month' in July 1979
- Certificate of award for five years of service
- Certificate of completion of the seminar 'The New Supervisor'
- Certificate of completion in 'Supervision'
- Certificate of completion in 'Managing People'
- Certificate of completion in 'Technical Instructor Training' at Howard Community College, Columbia, Maryland
- Ink Maker Magazine, showcased on front cover
- Certificate of award for 'Ten Years of Service'
- Certificate of completion in 'Printing Ink Course'
- Distinguished service award for 'Fifteen Years of Service'
- Distinguished service award for 'Twenty Years of Service'

My successful career with Graphic Fine Color, Inc. would not have been possible without the support and trust of the three individuals who saw me as a hard-working, dependable, reliable, and dedicated employee. They also noticed I was someone who was willing to give all my strength and effort to help the company succeed by making sure the departments for which I was responsible were always up to the task. In turn, they vowed to give me their support. They did everything humanly possible to help me succeed. I am deeply grateful to all of them. They are the founders and owners of Graphic Fine Color, Inc.

Stan G. Miller, CEO and Chairman of the Board

Harvey Ainbinder, President of Graphic Fine Color, Inc.

Robert T. Peters, Vice-President

Table of Contents

Introduction

Some stories must be carried.

Mine has been carried from the west coast of Africa, across the Atlantic Ocean, and halfway across America. I have carried it in my heart and mind for five decades, my entire life, and it has shaped my every choice.

I have shared my story with those I love, and now they carry it, too. I can recall countless nights with my wife, Evelyn Gail, who listened with great patience and care as I described emotional, often disturbing scenes from my past. We would lie awake together as I ran my mind over the brutal, strange memories, and she sometimes became so overcome with emotions that tears dropped from her eyes. My three children—now young adults themselves—heard my stories from the time they were very small. As they grew in body and mind, I revealed more of my past to them, unfolding my dark history and watching them absorb it curiously and eagerly. My family's understanding and acceptance have made it easier for me to move past the brutality that peppers my memories and focus on the joy that weaves in and out of them, like bright light snaking through fast-moving storm clouds.

Some stories must be carried. But when they are told, when they are released to eager listeners, they become lighter. Although I will carry my story for all of my living days, lately I have felt it pressing down upon me and I know the time has come to give it space and breath and a larger audience.

My story is not entirely unique, or unquestionably heroic, or universally inspiring. But it is a story full of adventure and wisdom, learning and loving, struggle and triumph. It illustrates how spending year after year struggling to survive can teach one to stand firm in all undertakings, regardless of counter influences, opposition, or discouragement. It proves that a determined, earnest boy from a poor farming community in Sierra Leone can fall, and rise, and travel, and change, and reinvent himself completely.

For more years than I can count, I intended to write a book about my experiences, starting in my childhood days and tracing my path to the present. Now, I have done it. Now you are reading it. Thank you for helping me to carry my story. I feel lighter already.

Chapter 1

A Life of Contradictions

When you think of Sierra Leone, what comes to your mind? Slave labor in cramped and deadly diamond mines? Constant political instability and frequent military coups? Child soldiers being recruited by ruthless warlords? Ebola, smallpox, and cholera epidemics creating wastelands of sickness? My homeland is one that has been ravaged by violence, disease, and greed, it's true. The country of my birth is a country of constant turmoil.

But I am the son of a midwife.

In my hometown of Robomp Bana—a remote village in the Northern Province of Sierra Leone—nearly all of the women are named after my mother, Yabu Kamara. She was the only midwife in our village, a small, undeveloped cluster of farms and community buildings that lacked hospitals, doctors, or nurses to care for the sick and suffering.

When a pregnant woman went into labor, although my mother would rush to be by her side, there was no sterile room for her to rush to or skilled physician to help her through her contractions. A baby might be delivered inside a mud-walled thatched house, in a hut or shed, deep in the woods, at the riverside, or wherever the woman happened to experience her labor pains.

My mother delivered dozens, possibly hundreds of babies during her lifetime, and all for free, as most of our neighbors lacked money to pay her. As a thank you for the work she did, the mothers named their baby girls after her. Even long after her death, her name is still given to new generations of women born in the village as a tribute to her memory.

I am also the son of a farmer.

In our village, farming was not an occupation but a way of life. Although a handful of my neighbors made their living as fishermen, nearly ninety percent of the village population worked as farmers. We had no tractors or reapers or threshers, but instead relied on simple manual labor and the power of our community to keep our farms thriving. We pulled weeds, hoed grass, sowed seeds, drove the birds away to stop them from eating the grain. If we weren't planting or harvesting crops, there was always wood to cut or collect for cooking, water to be fetched from wells or the seaside, eggs to gather, chickens to feed, sheep and goats led out to graze. When my brothers and I were feeling particularly enterprising, we'd use homemade slingshots to chase the birds or monkeys away from the crop fields.

In those fields, my father grew peanuts, cassava, and potatoes. Most crops grew on our upland farm about four miles from the village center, but we also had several acres of swamp farm where we grew rice. Most of what we grew was used to feed our own family, but when we had surplus crops we sold them to travelers or residents of other nearby villages. Coffee, kola nut, orange, coconut, avocado, and mango trees grew behind our house, and we harvested from them to further fill our family's dinner table.

It was a hard and simple life, but one that all of our neighbors understood and respected.

Despite the picture of simple poverty I have painted so far, I assure you that I am the son of a woman who was wealthy…in family.

In our village, a man is considered wealthy if the size of his farm is large or if he owned flocks of animals like cows, goats, sheep's and chickens. But a *woman's* status was measured by the number of children she had. I had nine brothers and sisters growing up, and a life rich in sibling fun and chaos.

I grew up devout because I am the son of an Imam.

My father, the Islamic leader of our village, taught the Quran to men, women, and children of all ages in the village. He also served as Imam and led the five daily prayers in the community mosque, a humble, two-room building constructed in the center of town. Our mosque was an important gathering place for everyone in the village, a community center where we worshipped daily but also celebrated on holy days and during festive weddings. And my father's presence made the mosque welcoming to all. He was a charismatic man despite being relatively uneducated, and he used his natural charm to exhort others to pray regularly. His influence was strong, and the habit quickly spread to neighboring villages.

In our household, observing the five daily prayers was as essential as eating. We were very fortunate in that physical hunger had never been an issue on my father's watch; he tended his farm carefully and strategically, so we always had plenty of rice and other foods to eat. My father was generous and jolly overall, but when it came to our religious practices, he was quite strict. His rule was that nothing came before prayers.

The first prayer of the day began in the early morning before daylight. Everyone in our household—with the exception of the very young or sick—was expected to be up and performing the rituals of purification before the sun rose. We would wash our faces first, then our mouths, noses, both arms, and both hands, then use our wet hands to moisten our heads. Finally, we would wash both feet in bowls of cool water drawn from our family well. Afterward, we were all expected to head promptly to the mosque for the morning prayer. My father was always the first person to wake up, and he took advantage of his natural tendency toward early rising. He'd go door to door, knocking and calling, instructing every resident of our village to wake up, wash up, and make their way to the mosque for prayers.

As for his own family members, he had limited patience for lethargy. If, after several attempts to wake us, we remained adamantly in bed, he usually filled a drinking cup with water and splashed it on the slothful person's unsuspecting face. The only way to avoid Dad's vengeful wake-up tactic was to get up *immediately* when he made his first call for morning prayers.

But aside from the occasional watery wake-up call, life in Robomp Bana was mostly quiet and relatively uneventful. We lived far from the diamond mines in a serene, agriculturally focused region, and when I was a child in the 1950s, the times of deep and violent political unrest were yet to arrive. We could walk from one village to the next given enough time and determination, but our village was only accessible by boat or canoe for anyone traveling a longer, non-walkable distance.

And we lived happily without most of the resources and conveniences associated with modern life. Just as we lacked doctors and modern medical care, our village was without a school. By the age of eight, I was actively helping my father with farming tasks, but could not read or write. There was no electricity in the village during my childhood, so kerosene camp lamps and a kind of homemade tin lamp called a "pan lamp" were our only light sources.

As you might imagine, we also lacked access to running water, refrigeration, or natural gas for cooking. When we needed to cook, we set a cooking pot atop three stones and placed wood for a fire underneath the pot. Since cooking was done outside, our "kitchens" were either in a shed with palm leaves roof at the back of the house, or a spot under a tree in an open backyard.

My childhood home was a mud house with a roof made from bamboo leaves, perched along the dirt road that connected our village to a few others in the Northern Province. During the dry season, the inside of the house was unbearably hot all day long, and only became tolerable at night when the cool sea breeze blew in. We spent most of the day outdoors anyway, tending the farm, cooking, or socializing.

When night fell, however, my whole family returned to the house to sleep. Our beds were handmade, with frames tied together by ropes and mattresses made from dry, soft grass covered with wraps or sheets. Over time the grass compressed and became hard and uncomfortable to sleep on, so we gradually added more. The constant drone and incessant pricking of mosquitoes could keep us all awake at times. Although my mother and father had a mesh tent over their bed to keep the mosquitoes out, the rest of us slept in tentless beds and dealt with endless miserable nights. My older brother and I shared a bed, and he would do his best to keep the mosquitoes at bay by fanning me with a piece of cloth while I slept. He was a caretaker by nature, more concerned about my safety than his own.

It's a good thing that most of my days were full to the brim with working tasks, because there was not much to do in the village for fun. The area in which my village was situated was beautiful country, and we were surrounded by trees, rivers, and infinite land, birds, monkeys and all kinds of animals. During the dry season especially, the sunshine made our surroundings look bright and beautiful. At night, the moon cast a pale, white light and sometimes my brothers and I would climb to the top of a tall hill to look at the rivers, farms, and forests in the surrounding areas. Beauty was everywhere, but beautiful landscapes only held the attention of a growing boy for so long.

Although I spent most of my time with my siblings, I also developed a group of rowdy friends from neighboring family farms. They were all good-natured but also a little bit wild, always looking for adventure, and extremely fond of climbing trees. Since we had a cluster of tall fruit and nut trees behind my parents' house, my gang of friends loved to meet up there and challenge each other to climbing contests.

I was not an expert tree climber like my friends, who could (and would) climb any tree of any height within minutes. I longed to be as brave and agile as the others, but

I was afraid of heights…and I couldn't shake the memory of a terrifying experience I'd had while climbing a kola nut tree.

One late afternoon, after a short day working in the fields, my friends and I were playing a version of hide-and-go-seek in my backyard. I decided to climb up the kola nut tree to hide from them, but when I got halfway up the tree, I froze. A vibrant green snake peered at me coldly from between the branches. It was folded around itself like a garden hose, with its head lying on top of a thick coil and its black tongue flicking in and out, in and out. The moment the snake sensed movement, it lifted its head slowly and brought it level with my own, locking its sinister yellow eyes with mine. Then it began to unfold itself and stretched its long, lithe, green body out on the branches. It was the longest snake I had ever seen.

According to my fellow villagers, tree-dwelling green snakes were supposed to be friendly. And although this particular green snake didn't offer to become my lifelong pal, it made no move to strike or hurt me. Instead, it sized me up silently, turned its head, and moved away from me. Nevertheless, I panicked; I was so terrified that I let go of the branch I was holding, fell out of the tree, and landed hard on my left shoulder. The pain when I landed on the ground was excruciating, and I cried out for my friends to come out of hiding to help me. They appeared immediately—frightened themselves but galvanized into action—lifted me and carried me inside the house to my mother.

When she saw my tiny injured body being carried toward her, my poor mother passed out instantly. She'd seen a lot of pain and strife as a midwife, but the sight of her own dear boy prone and moaning in pain was too much for her. As she lay on the ground quietly sweating, two of her women friends who were in the house with her took off their head ties and fanned her with them.

When my mother regained consciousness and calmed down enough to comprehend what had happened, she quickly ran to the woods and picked some leaves that she knew had pain-controlling properties. She brought them into the house, ground them with a wooden mortar, and added a little water to form a paste. She then rubbed the healing salve on my shoulder. As it slowly dried, I felt the area tighten which caused the pain to lessen. My shoulder was sore for a couple of days, but that didn't stop me from going to the farm and working once I was up on my feet again.

It did, however, stop me from climbing trees. I was earthbound for life after that disastrous encounter with the friendly green snake.

Another of our limited entertainment options was swimming in nearby rivers and ponds, which my gang of friends loved to do. Unless someone was sick or had some important personal event to attend to, we had no regular days off from working the farmland. But occasionally we would get lucky and work a shorter day, then have the afternoon off to play and explore. When this happened, my friends inevitably ended up down by the river, eager to splash about in the water.

Over time, I became an excellent swimmer…but not by choice.

One sunny, beautiful afternoon during the dry season, my friends and I were headed home from a morning's work harvesting rice in the swamp. Everyone wanted to cool off by swimming in the river, and although I was only about eight years old and unable to swim at the time, I agreed to join them. My other option was to head home alone to entertain myself, so I figured I would watch from the riverbanks or maybe splash a little in the shallows. My friend Sorieba was also unable to swim, so I knew I'd have company.

Everyone removed their clothes before swimming, and since neither I nor Sorieba joined in the watery fun, it was our job to keep an eye on our friends' clothing while they swam. Our group of friends was never the only one crowding into the river, and boys of all ages from our village gathered there to enjoy some time in the cool, gently flowing water. It was a raucous scene, and even though Sorieba and I had to watch from afar while guarding everyone's clothing, we enjoyed being near the action.

On this particular afternoon, our friends had put together a secret plan that would force me and Sorieba to brush up on our swimming skills. The idea was to push the two of us into the river, then rescue us right away before panic set in. Our expert-swimmer friends were convinced it would be a hilarious joke, and successfully prevented us from discovering their sneaky plan.

The two of us sat together, quietly talking, on a high ridge of the riverbank sheltered by a tree and bordering a section of the river that was surprisingly deep. Two of our friends tiptoed up behind us and pushed us hard so we flew past the sandy banks, throwing our flailing bodies into the deep, still water.

It all happened so quickly, I didn't even have time to shout or struggle, and I soon felt myself sinking rapidly toward the muddy river bottom. I opened my eyes but could only see murky water with bits of plants and soil floating about, and I began to feel the pressure of my held breath pressing against my chest. The push had been so fast and forceful that I hadn't had a chance to breathe deeply before I hit the water, and I was rapidly running out of air. I clumsily kicked myself toward the surface as fast as I could, confused and frightened, and surfaced to see the grinning face of Amadu, the oldest of us.

"Well, Ansu, at least you didn't just sink like a stone. Maybe now you'll learn to swim properly!" he exclaimed as he towed me back toward the shore.

Sorieba had floated a bit further downstream, but another of the boys had followed him into the water and pulled him out quickly. Neither of us was hurt, but the incident had been completely terrifying.

"You think that was funny?" Sorieba shouted. "You idiots! We could have died!"

"Don't be a big baby, Sorieba," said our friend Sheka, giving him a playful shove. "We had it under control. We weren't going to let you two drown. Just wanted to teach you a lesson."

"Yeah, and that lesson is: Learn to swim!" added Baisama.

And so we did.

Since we knew we'd never be safe perched on the riverbanks guarding everyone else's clothes, Sorieba and I forced ourselves to practice swimming on the shallow side of the river. Our rambunctious friends were too busy entertaining themselves to help us out, so the learning went slowly. But by watching and mimicking them, we eventually learned to float, then swim, then dive gracefully into the water from the high banks. It felt good to be able to join the group fully as they frolicked in the water on blazing hot afternoons. But we never quite forgave our buddies for tricking us into becoming expert swimmers.

And when our unattended clothes got swiped by other troops of boys, we always made sure to rub it in. If only Sorieba and I had been left alone to guard everyone's belongings...

* * *

Our life was full of extremes: The punishing wet season and blazing-hot dry season. The richness of the harvest balanced by months when food became scarce. The intensity of hard farm labor offset by long hours of empty, unstructured time.

Our life was also full of contradictions: we were unimaginably poor, but never felt lacking and knew we were rich in love. We were isolated in a remote part of the country 100 miles from the capital city of Freetown, but constantly surrounded by neighbors and community members eager to help and support us. We were largely uneducated but guided by the wisdom of our elders and sustained by the insights of our faith.

It was a hard life. A simple life. And its mixture of extremes and contradictions created a kind of elegant balance that helped me grow strong and sharp, curious and inquisitive as I absorbed the harsh abundance of the world around me.

Chapter 2

Seasons and Cycles of Life

Like so many children, most of my memories are packed with people: My parents and siblings in scenes from life in our shared home, my group of rambunctious but loyal friends making mayhem, my fellow villagers gathering at the mosque for prayer. But my young life was also influenced by my surroundings, by the land, by the natural forces that created and continue to shape my home country of Sierra Leone.

City dwellers may idly discuss the weather to pass the time or create "small talk" with strangers, but farmers view heat waves and cold fronts quite differently. When you make your living off of the land, storms, heat, rain, drought, and the changing of the seasons shape your world in direct and unavoidable ways. Farmers and their families live their lives at the mercy of the elements. My family was no exception.

Although the climate in virtually all of Sierra Leone is considered tropical and temperatures seldom drop below 70°F, the country does experience distinct seasons. The dry season typically stretched from November to April, and although this period lacked rainfall it brought other challenges. The rainy season took over from May to November, and the weather during this time could be hot, humid, wet, and miserable. Frequently, the month of August would bring long, intense days of rain to Sierra Leone. We planted our crops during the rainy season to take advantage of the moist soil and nourishing water, but depending on how rainy it truly was, we had to adjust our work schedules accordingly!

Although both rainy and dry seasons could be frustrating at times, both were also important to the harvest cycle. Farmers generally saw the good in the dry season as a time of harvest and bounty, and the good in the rainy season as a time of planting and tremendous growth.

But farmers and non-farmers alike dreaded *Harmattan.*

Sierra Leone lies in the path of the legendary *Harmattan* wind, which blows from the Sahara Desert over the West African subcontinent into the Gulf of Guinea. *Harmattan* season isn't exactly like winter, since temperatures remain fairly warm, but the wind is strong, harsh, and drying, bringing with it a dusty haze that sweeps over the landscape. The wind does cut the humidity and since it arrives during the months when Sierra Leone gets the least amount of sunlight, it is during this time period that we harvested our crops and prepared the fields for a few months of dormancy.

But *Harmattan* is harsh on both plants and people. The dry, dusty wind causes sudden temperature fluctuations. A morning that began cool and pleasant may suddenly become hot and stuffy. *Harmattan* also caused health issues for the people of Sierra Leone. The relentless dryness brings widespread skin irritation and itching, dry painful eyes, and frequent nosebleeds. I myself dealt with raw, painful skin and incessant bloody noses as a child when *Harmattan* rolled through my village. Although some people were more tolerant of its effects, no one was truly immune to the wind's erosive power. We would all grit our teeth to make it through this unpleasant annual event.

Since planting season began after several months of living off crops from the most recent harvest, many families ran out of rice by early May. Farmers who needed rice to plant and grow during the approaching rainy season typically borrowed it from families who'd been lucky enough to harvest a surplus and still had rice to spare. Our community was small and trusting, so this type of arrangement was never considered shameful or stressful, simply a natural part of rural life. That said, the family who needed to borrow rice was always grateful and expected to pay back the loan with interest. Once the next harvest rolled around, the amount paid back was normally double the amount borrowed. (If a farmer borrowed one bag of rice during the planting season, the payback would be two bags.) Our family farm was often quite bountiful, so in addition to our land's annual yield, my father often collected rice that other farmers had borrowed from us during the shortage period.

Including me, my mother and father had ten children, and every single one of us depended upon the farm for our daily meals as well as our standard of living. My father devoted all of his youth and adult life to farming and over time—as we observed the pride and care he took in tending our family's land—my siblings and I began to understand what being a farmer truly meant. Farming is hard work, especially when there is no machinery to aid in the endless

27

labor. My father owned and operated 20 acres of land and swamp farm combined, and made it clear to me and my brothers and sisters that watching the farm thrive was his life's work. Being able to provide for our entire family made him so happy. Our annual yield mostly went directly toward feeding the family, with only a little left over to sell for profit, so it did not make us wealthy per se. But we were able to live healthy lives free of hunger and without struggle. My father's ability to support his family and help those in need of crops during the shortage period lent our family prominence and recognition within our community.

Our farm produced abundant crops each year and was especially successful at growing rice which was our staple food and main crop. We also did well growing peanuts, a crop that had many uses. Peanut butter was a staple food in our household, and my parents would also make peanut oil which was our main type of cooking oil. Potatoes were a smaller crop for us, but since they survived many months in storage without rotting and could be prepared in so many ways, they helped round out our family meals.

Our cassava plantation was also abundant, and we used every part of the plant we possibly could. Cassava leaves are edible when chopped or ground, and my mother used to make a cassava leaf soup that was eaten with rice. The roots of the cassava plant are its main crop, and when the skin is peeled off and the root is ground up, it creates a thick, starchy paste that's similar to mashed potatoes. Fufu—a doughy side dish made from mashed cassava—is a staple for many West African families. Next to rice, fufu was my parent's favorite food, and my mother cooked it at least twice a week using a simple but tasty recipe she'd learned from her own mother.

Our home was situated in the village, about four miles from our agricultural fields, so the mango, orange, avocado, and coconut trees that grew in our yard offered us additional food for the family table much closer to home. We had fruit for breakfast nearly every day and used these flavorful items to season our meals. Some of our surplus farm crops were sold or traded, but the delicious fruit that grew in our backyard was for my family to enjoy amongst ourselves.

Cooking and food preparation was usually done by my sisters, under the watchful eye of my mother. I had four mischievous sisters who didn't contribute to the hard labor of planting and harvesting alongside us six boys, but they worked hard to make our meals. They were also a sly group who had no pity on their male siblings, always finding ways to make us work even harder once we'd returned from the day's farming tasks!

The boys—especially the younger ones—would often sit around the cooking area and watch the girls work to prepare our meals. My sisters found this bothersome, claiming our presence was a distraction. We would often see them whispering amongst themselves, clearly hatching some plan to get us out from under their feet.

My sister Isatu would often end up saying, "Guys, we don't have enough wood to cook everything today. We need you to go out and gather more wood."

What could we do? We'd traipse out into the woods and to gather and cut down dry branches. Once we hauled our findings back to the cooking area, my sister Marie would say, "Boys, we've only got one drum of water. Head down to the well and bring us some more, or we'll never get this meal done!"

The well was at least a quarter mile from the house, not exactly a quick trip. And hauling water was hard, bothersome work. But our sisters were insistent, so we'd start heading down toward the well to do as they'd ask.

On our way back, we often saw them giggling together, pointing and laughing as we labored. These errands they sent us on were often unnecessary: They likely had plenty of wood and water to finish their cooking tasks. This was just their way of getting us out of their way and tricking us into doing more work. They found this hilarious, and we found it infuriating. But we were at their mercy. If we refused, they might claim that a late or unfinished meal was our fault for not pitching in. Whatever tricks they pulled, we had to oblige them or risk empty stomachs and a wrathful mother.

Of course, farm life wasn't just about coping with the weather or enjoying the bounty of the fields at dinner time. We worked hard nearly every day to keep the crops healthy and the farm thriving. Unless someone was sick or had an important family matter to attend to, we had no regular days off, no weekends to rest and relax. Occasionally, the weather or holidays would create the opportunity to work a shorter day, and when this happened my friends and I would inevitably end up playing by the river. But such days were few and far between. Our working activities varied day by day as well as season by season, but there was never a shortage of work that needed doing.

Early every morning, when the roosters crowed before dawn, my father and brothers awoke and gathered together to walk to the fields. Our upland farm was outside the village and set apart from our house, as were several acres of swamp farm we used for growing rice. We walked for about an hour every morning to arrive at the farm, and another hour at the end of the day to get back home.

When we headed off to work in the morning, we walked in single file along the narrow dirt roads. Since we left home before daylight, the person at the front of the line held a flickering kerosene camp lamp to help us see our way along the unlit road. Raucous monkeys and cooing pigeons were wide awake and active at dawn, so there was plenty of ruckus to keep us awake as we made our slow way toward the fields.

The men headed to the farm before dawn to begin working the land, and the women normally followed later. We measured time by the movement of the sun, and when the sun was directly overhead, a party of women would leave the village and head for the fields, bringing food and water to the farmers for their mid-day meal.

Everyone stopped working briefly to eat and socialize once the food arrived. After we'd gobbled up every morsel that our mother and sisters had brought, we might sing and talk with each other for a little while, then head back to work. The singing and joking was short-lived, but important, since it helped break up the day. Without a lunchtime rest period in which to laugh and tell stories, work on the farm could feel dull, slow, and repetitive, so we were always grateful and excited when the troop of women arrived for our communal lunch break.

As you may have guessed, women's role on the farm was mostly supportive. Although my mother and sisters also participated in the planting and harvesting of our crops, they were not as involved in the heavy labor as my father, my brothers, and myself. Like the other village women, my mother and sisters were mainly responsible for cooking and distribution of food, as well as hauling water jugs out to the laborers to cool their throats during the hot, dry harvest season.

As farmers, we always appreciated rainfall, knowing it would help our crops grow and thrive. But whenever it began to rain as we were working the land, we had no choice but to continue our tasks while gradually becoming soaked to the bone. We had no shelter or cover in the fields, so if it was raining during our lunch break, we simply ate in the downpour. I remember one long day during the rainy season when we'd been working in the fields until at least 1 p.m., keeping a watchful eye on the dark overcast sky, when our mother and sisters finally arrived with the midday meal.

"It's been dry all morning," my father said. "But we need to eat quickly. I don't like the look of those clouds. It will start raining any minute, I think."

Sure enough, the moment we started dishing the food into bowls, we heard the pitter-patter of raindrops. By the time we had all been served, the sprinkle had turned to a heavy downpour. As we sat on the ground, soaking wet and eating our increasingly watered-down food, the only positive thought I could summon was that I was there with my loving family, not alone. And as I looked at the faces of my brothers and sisters and both my parents, I saw that no one was angry or frowning. In fact, they all wore quiet smiles. Looking back, I think of this as exemplifying the life of a farmer: Take what comes to you and make the best of it. Bad moods and complaints never help get the work done any faster.

Before planting season began, we had to deal with the grassy brush that grew up during the dry season. Once it had reached its full height and began to die out from lack of water, we allowed the brush to dry out for about a month, and then we used a controlled burning technique to get rid of it. When the fires had died out and the brush was cool, we cleared the land manually. Although the clearing was prickly and dirty work, I always enjoyed watching the brush smolder in the dancing orange flames. My father kept a watchful eye on the controlled burn, but I could tell that he, too, enjoyed the wild beauty of the fire.

My father had mastered some controlled burning techniques, but fire is unpredictable and can take unexpected paths. This happened one year when we were burning away the brush on our upland farm. We all knew that starting a fire on a windy day was ill-advised, but also that there is some inherent competition in farming. Every farmer wants to be the first to finish for the season, so every farmer pushes the timing of each stage whenever he can. I cannot remember if my father and brothers had chosen to risk setting a controlled burn on a breezy day, trying to get ahead of their work a bit, or if other factors were at play. But this fire grew large and uncontrollable quickly, and began to make its way toward a neighbor's lands before we knew what was happening.

We had no fire department, no fire extinguishers, and no real tools to bring the fire back under our control. All we could do was attempt to keep it from spreading further, halt its blazing progress. And we got lucky: This rebellious fire didn't end up damaging any growing crops on our neighbor's farm. In fact, since we all undertook the brush-burning tasks around the same time, our fire may have actually helped get our neighbor's clearing work done!

But even if that fire had done more harm than good, there would have been no ill will. All of the farmers in my village worked in harmony, knowing that peace and understanding within their community was essential. They all did the same types of work at the same time, all understood each other's needs and struggles, all pitched in to help when any single farmer was in trouble. If one farmer tries to burn his own brush and the fire leaps across to another farm, this is no crime or offense. The farmers viewed such incidents as part of a complex process that bound them all together. No one was happy when damage was incurred, but no bad blood was created, either.

Once the land was clear, we entered the plowing phase, using handheld hoes to prepare the soil for planting. Since our farm was fairly large at 20 acres, plowing could take several weeks to complete. When the land was completely plowed we then started sowing the rice seeds in both the upland and swamp farm. After the rice seeds were sown, the planting of peanuts, cassava, potatoes and other crops immediately followed.

Since planting took place during the rainy season, there was no need to irrigate the land. Water fell from the sky all day and all night sometimes, so we relied on the weather to keep our crops from getting thirsty.

Ten children may sound like a lot, but we felt lucky to have such a large family to help distribute the never-ending farm tasks. Other families sometimes struggled to keep up with their daily duties, especially during the height of planting and harvesting seasons. Smaller families often didn't have enough people to help complete the needed work, especially if their farms grew a variety of crops. If a family had too few people helping out, some of their crops might not get planted or harvested in a timely fashion. And despite the fact that everyone in our household participated in farm work, even our large family fell behind a few times and was unable to complete the work on time.

Luckily, my village upheld the tradition of mutual help.

Mutual help was an agreement between families to pitch in and help neighbors on a rotating basis. Farmers who were participating would agree on a schedule: All available workers would work together on one particular farm on a given day, then move on to a different farm the following day and continue until all members of the group had their turn. It was understood that the participant whose farm was being worked on any given day would provide food for all of the workers. They did this gladly since the mutual help arrangement kept their crops from failing.

Sharing labor was helpful to individual families, but also kept our community close-knit and happy. At night, especially during the dry season, it was customary for multiple families in the village to build a large wood fire and gather everyone around it. We called these family gathering nights and would spend hours watching the wood burn down and adding more to keep it roaring into the night sky. We ate boiled peanuts, sang traditional songs, and got to know each other better.

Nearly everyone in the village looked forward to family gathering nights. Those long companionable evenings were often spent telling stories of all kinds. Some of the stories were laugh-out-loud funny and brought joy to all who heard them. Other stories were sad and somber, filling our eyes with tears and our hearts with sorrow.

One such story stands out in my mind, a memory of an incident in 1960.

The Islamic faith requires its followers to fast from dawn until dusk for 29 or 30 days during the month of Ramadan. At the end of this period, there is a massive celebration called the day of Eid. During Ramadan in 1960, I remember seeing a large group of people leave my village one morning, and I asked my mother what was happening.

"They are traveling to Freetown by boat to shop in preparation for the day of Eid feast," she told me.

"Why aren't you going with them?" I asked.

"We have plenty here to make a good meal for you and your brothers and sisters," she said. "I didn't feel like I needed to buy anything extra this year."

We were lucky my mother made this choice.

On the way back home, our townspeople's boat encountered some bad weather. A violent storm with gusting winds and merciless rain pounded the vessel and tossed its passengers around. It was so overfilled with passengers that one strong wave threw it off balance. The boat capsized suddenly, dumping dozens of helpless people into the deep sea. The boat itself was large enough to trap many underneath, and between the boat's bulk, the throngs of people thrashing underwater together, and the brutal storm, few could find their way back to the surface. Those who did, had little hope of being rescued. Many died, including our neighbors and friends.

And if that terrible news wasn't bad enough, the tides brought worse to our village: Dead bodies were washed towards us by the waves, floating to shore on the beaches around my village. I remember seeing women and men I'd known my whole life, now lifeless themselves, glassy-eyed and swollen with seawater. It was a horrific scene, especially so for young children like me, and no one ever forgot it. The day of Eid was supposed to be a day of joyful celebration, but that year it turned to a day of sorrow and loss we would never forget. Its story was told on family gathering nights so we could remember those we'd lost, and comfort those left behind.

In addition to telling and sharing stories, family gathering nights were when the past, present, and future activities in the village were discussed. If a specific issue arose that needed addressing, all those involved would gather along with a highly respected community member to serve as mediator. One of the most common issues that arose would be when one farmer began to plant crops deep into another farmer's lands without first securing permission. The mediator would listen to testimony from both sides and attempt to create a settlement that would be relatively agreeable to all. Sometimes this would be a simple apology, other times a small fine. If a settlement could not be peaceably reached, the matter would be reported to the chief of the village who would undertake a detailed review of the matter himself. He might even visit the disputed area in person to see where the land's divisions fell. If the chief felt there wasn't enough evidence to support the assertion that wrong had been done, he would dismiss the issue. But if evidence was present, he would set a fine in either money or bags of rice. The fine was required to be paid off within a certain timeframe, set by the chief.

In addition to keeping family ties strong and providing a time to relax after a hard day's work, family gathering night was also a time when minor disputes were settled. If there was an argument between two family members or an issue between two people from different families, and they could not settle it among themselves, the matter was brought to the family gathering nights to be settled by the elders.

Many disputes were between siblings who could not agree on how to get a certain task accomplished or problem dealt with. Others were contentious arguments or issues of jealousy. Perhaps one family member felt that she or he was getting less attention from the parents than a sibling. These feelings may seem harmless, but they can fester into rivalry, and eventually lead to malice. Often, the sibling who feels neglected isn't the one to bring the issue to the gathering. Another family member who has observed the dynamic would mention it, asking the elders to intervene and settle the dispute. Any issue that was settled at family gathering—small or big, minor or major—was respected by all. And it was incredibly helpful to everyone to have a reasonable and universally respected peacekeeping group to help us work through challenging family disputes.

As the dusty, dry *Harmattan* swept through my village, licking at the bonfire and tickling our ears, we laughed and shared and learned together. And when the rains came and drove us back to our separate homes, we missed those long nights spent in the company of our wise and wily fellow villagers.

Chapter 3

A Family Crisis

Fathers are complex and significant figures. They can be gentle or harsh, fair or unpredictable, nurturing or frightening. And their temperaments and parenting styles shape the lives of their children in ways they may never fully comprehend.

I was extremely fortunate to have a level-headed, loving, and wise father. As I've mentioned, he served as Imam to our entire town and our neighbors trusted him to resolve disputes and conflicts since he was fair-minded and impartial, never showing favoritism or bias. Everyone liked and respected him, looking to him for wisdom and guidance.

His public persona was as one of the most trustworthy and revered men in our community, but there were aspects of his personality that he only showed at home. My father was the type of man who adored laughter and mischief. It brought him such joy to play little practical jokes on his children, or tell silly stories that would make us all laugh until the tears streamed down from our eyes.

At family gathering nights, he was serious more often than not, but occasionally he would let his fun-loving side shine through. I remember one night when I was very young, hearing him tell a story that showed everyone around the fire how sneaky he could be when he set his mind to it. It seems that when he was younger, my father and two of his friends decided to go rabbit hunting. They set off together from the village, but on arrival at the spot they knew to be best for catching rabbits, they decided to split up. They set a time to meet back at that same location, planning to compare their kills of the day and see who had caught more rabbits.

Once they were reunited, my father insisted that his two friends talk about their kills before him. His first friend proclaimed he had nabbed four rabbits. The second friend proudly stated that he'd killed five rabbits. My father puffed out his chest and declared he'd snagged a whopping six rabbits that afternoon and waited to see how impressed and surprised his friends were…before revealing he'd really only gotten two rabbits that day. He loved studying people's reactions and would say just about anything to get a rise out of them.

This included my mother. She was a calm, even-keeled woman overall, but my father really knew how to press her buttons. If she showed preference for a certain dress or pair of shoes, he'd hide them from her. Then watch gleefully as she turned the house upside-down searching for them. Once he'd enjoyed watching her become more frantic and frustrated by the minute, he'd take the items from their hiding place and return them to her. I witnessed this game a few times throughout my childhood, and it was a sight to see.

"What is WRONG with you, Sulaiman? Are you trying to drive me mad?" I remember her asking him one time, after a particularly long and enraging search for her favorite brown dress.

My father laughed his musical laugh and replied, "I'm just trying to keep you on your toes! Laugh, Yabu. Be happy like me."

She rolled her eyes at him but smiled ruefully as she stalked off to put on her newly retrieved dress.

When I was about nine years old, my father was in his 60s and age began to take its toll on his mind and body. He became tired more easily and had to do less and less hard labor on the farm. Luckily, my older brother, Abu, had worked closely with my dad over the years and stepped easily into the role of "head of the household."

Abu was the second child to be born to our parents, and the oldest male out of ten children in our family, which made him the logical successor to my father. As a child, he had been full of energy and imagination, traits that matured into curiosity and charisma over time. Farming had been the only occupation offered to him, so Abu did his best to adapt and learn the skills he needed to do it well. Gradually, he also took on my father's role as community leader, working the farm by day and overseeing family gathering nights in the evening. He, too, was considered trustworthy and wise, always remaining neutral and giving sound, helpful advice. He filled my father's shoes naturally and fully, quickly becoming a reliable farm manager and pillar of the community. By the time I was nine years old, he had come into his own as a village leader.

But shortly after he had stepped fully into his role as household head and community advisor, Abu became mysteriously ill. One evening toward the end of the rainy season, after a long day's labor, he complained of a throbbing headache and backache. He went to bed early, hoping to sleep it off. But the following morning, his pain was worse, and he had become feverish. Shortly after waking, he began vomiting frequently and violently, which added exhaustion and dehydration to his list of ailments. He was in a bad way and had to stay in bed to recover.

Abu's illness brought farming and all other productive activities to a standstill. Without my father or Abu to lead and guide us, my siblings and mother felt paralyzed and a little bit afraid.

Then things got worse.

By the second day of his illness, Abu had developed angry-looking blisters all over his body. His skin was raw and inflamed, and soon his sores erupted with pus. These symptoms were familiar to us—having seen other villagers suffering from them in the past—and they filled everyone in my family with dread. My older brother was infected with one of the deadliest diseases mankind has ever known: smallpox.

When my mother broke the news to my father, he said, "Our poor son is suffering, and it breaks my heart. I wish I were strong enough to take on some of his work and duties, but I simply cannot. I'm old and weak and sick myself."

He took a slow, racking breath and looked into my mother's eyes.

"Yabu, you are head of the household for now."

And so leadership fell to my mother. She now had to look after all of her 10 children, nurse her husband, keep the farm from falling into disuse, and attempt to save her son from a lethal disease. Her own mother, my maternal grandmother, had come to visit a few weeks previously and once the news of Abu's illness broke, she decided to stay and help. But even with the support of her mother, my own mother was overwhelmed and afraid. She steeled herself, focused and determined to do everything in her power to protect her family. Her whole family.

"Have faith, Ansu," she told me when I confessed my own fears. She placed her cool, dry hand on my cheek. "We will make it through this."

Despair lurked in the shadows of our household during that dark time, but my mother's faith gave me faith.

We lacked any modern medical facility in our own village but taking him to Freetown was financially impossible. We could not afford to travel back and forth multiple times, nor did we have the money to pay for medical treatment in the city. But since his oozing blisters were plainly visible, no passenger boat would've taken us on anyway, so it didn't really matter that we were too poor to get him to Freetown for help.

Knowing this, my mother considered her limited options. Time was running out for my brother who was suffering and in constant pain. As smallpox progresses, lesions begin to appear inside the nose and mouth. As this began to happen to Abu, his eyes would water constantly from the intensity of his pain. He was weak and feverish, so he seldom spoke, but all of my siblings and I would peer into his room, terrified, as he thrashed and groaned on his hard, straw bed. When the pale sunlight fell through the open window onto his skin, we could see it was gnarled with sores, painfully leaking fluid and draining away his very life.

After a few days, my mother decided it would be best to take my brother away from our village. Since my dad was in a delicate state himself, she feared that keeping Abu at home might overtax his weakened system. Dad knew that his oldest son, whom he expected to take over the affairs of the family, was also in poor health. But watching Abu deteriorate might push him over the edge into panic or despair. The last thing my mother wanted was to lose my father, too.

My siblings and I had taken to loitering near the mango trees behind our house. We'd gather there to worry and whisper in the afternoons. One day as we were milling around, kicking at the dust and wondering what to do with ourselves, my mother came striding out.

"You are NOT to discuss your brother's condition with your father, do you understand?" she said firmly, wagging a finger at us. "He is worried enough as it is. Don't make it worse by talking with him about Abu. Promise me."

She didn't need to be so stern. We were all anxious and afraid and had no desire to upset our dad.

"What are we going to do, Mom?" asked my sister, Mabinti.

"I have decided to take Abu to Rokoya, where my father lives. If we can get there, I believe he can help us find a healer. We cannot stay here any longer. Your grandmother will help while we are gone."

Rokoya was a ten-mile trip; the first two miles were spent crossing a wide river and the remaining eight miles had to be walked. It was a long journey, but my mother felt it was her only hope of curing her son. She decided to take me along to help with her bags, freeing her up to hold my brother by his shoulder, help him walk, inch by inch, slowly, and painfully. I was only nine at the time, but already active, smart, and fairly fearless. Because of my disposition and eager nature, my parents often asked for my help with important tasks. And I took them all very seriously.

I will never forget that trip. It was incredibly tedious, but tense and frightening at the same time. We set out just after our dawn prayers. I carried two handmade bags and a plastic jar of water. One of the bags contained our clothing and the other one had mangos, bananas and plums to eat along the road. My mother propped up Abu and coaxed him along. To get to Rokoya we had to head north, which meant crossing the river just outside Robomp Bana. A family friend was kind enough to take us across the two-mile wide stretch of water on his boat, keeping a wary distance from Abu and covering his mouth with a piece of cloth as he poled us all across the water. Once we made it to the other side, we thanked him, and the three of us began to make our slow way along mud roads and through treacherous swamps. The air was thick with heat and the clatter of insects.

My brother did not have the energy to walk very far without resting, so we stopped frequently. I was grateful since our bags felt heavy on my skinny 9-year-old frame, but my mother was anxious and fretting. She would mop

Abu's brow with a rag as he leaned, panting, against fallen logs or towering trees, her gaze constantly scanning the horizon. We were far from home and far from help. She worried about crocodiles in the swamps and rivers, worried about snakes in the brush and forest, worried about getting stuck outside walking should a heavy rain begin to fall. Whenever she caught me looking at her, she would smile weakly.

"It's OK, Ansu," she'd tell me, her voice shaky. "Just keeping an eye out."

But her worry began to worry me. I found myself feeling jumpy and fearful the longer we walked.

And we walked for a long, long time.

There are two other villages situated between our village and Rokoya. After walking all day and stopping frequently to rest under shady trees, we made it to the first village by nightfall. As the sun's last rays ducked behind the horizon, we stumbled, exhausted into the tiny town. There, my mother sought shelter for the night at an old friend of hers. We were incredibly lucky that this lady offered us a room in the back of her thatched house. She even gave us straw mats to spread on the floor since there were no beds in the room.

But the night was long and miserable. We had no nets to protect us from the mosquitoes, and they attacked relentlessly. I could hear Abu thrashing about in the darkness. He tried so valiantly to hide his suffering, but occasionally a dry moan escaped his cracked lips. My mother must have stayed awake all night, because every time Abu would moan, she would huff or sigh. Her worry was thick in the tiny room, like a heavy but invisible fog settling over all three of us.

We had no rest that night.

The next morning, just before dawn, my mother thanked her friend for allowing us to spend the night and we continued on. Despite our lack of sleep, lying still for the night had given Abu a bit more strength, and the morning passed fairly quickly. My mother could sense when he was wearing out, and checked in frequently.

"Do you want to stop?" she'd ask, peering into his haggard face.

"No," he replied hoarsely, "not yet."

But soon enough he would tire. We would find a shady spot, I would set down our bags, and we'd sit for 15 minutes or so until Abu raised his head.

"I'm ready," he'd say, his voice dull and scratchy.

As young as I was, I knew that he was being brave and strong. His eyes were glazed over, his steps dragging, and he still would not allow himself to sit for too long. He knew we had to make it to help soon or it would mean his end.

We walked and walked and rested and walked, on again and off again, finally passing the second village by late afternoon. By evening we finally arrived at Rokoya.

As soon as we entered my grandfather's house, my mother cried out.

"Father!" she said, her eyes welling up.

My grandfather's smile, his delight on seeing us, quickly evaporated as he saw the look on her face. He stood quickly from where he sat near the cooking fire and ran to meet her. They embraced tightly.

"But what is the matter, Yabu?" he inquired, placing his rough hand against her cheek. She looked over at Abu, who stood leaning weakly against the doorway.

Grandfather nodded knowingly. He could see the angry blisters on Abu's skin in the fading twilight, and his own face went tight with worry.

"Do not worry. I will fetch Bokari Nufu right away," he told us. And without another word, he grabbed his walking stick, and hurried out the front door.

I saw a single tear roll down my mother's dark face, but she also sighed with relief. We had made it. Help was on the way. Abu would be all right. Bokari Nufu was the most trusted healer for miles around, gifted in creating cures from herbs and roots. We were in the clear.

About half an hour later, my grandfather padded back into the house with a powerful looking man in his fifties trailing behind. Bokari Nufu had an air of wisdom and authority about him, and it filled the room like a scent when he entered. My mother was trembling with anticipation. All her hopes rested on this man.

"Well, Yabu, let's have a look at this son of yours," he said in a rich baritone voice.

"Yes, of course," she said. "He is resting in the back room. I'll take you."

The three adults filed out, leaving me alone to poke idly at the cooking fire.

I would later learn that Bokari Nufu had learned the art of healing techniques from his grandfather, who had also been a native healer and roots specialist. At Rokoya and neighboring villages, Bokari Nufu renowned for his ability to treat and often cure chronic diseases, as well as help ease people through short-term illness. I could just barely hear my mother answering his questions in the next room, and edged closer to the doorway.

"It is smallpox, you are right. And it's one of the worst cases I've ever seen," said Bokari Nufu. "But you know, around Rokoya, they say that the only ones who don't survive smallpox are the ones who haven't been treated my me!"

My mother laughed nervously.

"Yes, of course! We are so lucky that you've agreed to help my dear son," she spluttered. "Is there any way to ease his pain now?"

I crept closer, peeking around the doorway into the gradually darkening back bedroom.

Bokari Nufu reached for his soft animal skin medicine bag and took out a tiny brown glass vial full of an herbal brew of some sort. He brought it toward my brother's bed and knelt down.

"Drink this, Abu," he rumbled in his dark, rich voice.

And Abu did. Gratefully and quickly. Then he rested his head back and took a deep breath. I knew he was praying, hoping against hope that whatever he had just swallowed would lessen his suffering.

"We'll start by giving him large, regular doses of herbal medicines by mouth. This will treat the sickness from the inside," he explaincd. "Once he's made some progress, possibly after a day or two, I'll start treating the sores on his body."

My mother nodded quickly and wordlessly. My grandfather held her arm, and it was hard to tell which one was giving strength and which one was taking it.

"Wake him twice tonight and give him one bottle each time," said Bokari Nufu, pressing two more tiny bottles into my mother's hand. "I'll be back tomorrow to check on him."

And with that, he swept out of the room, passing me in the bedroom doorway, and striding out the front. I turned to watch but he was gone in a flash.

As I turned back, I saw that my mother was kneeling next to my brother's bed, pressing a cloth to his head as tears flowed silently down her cheeks and onto the dirt floor. My grandfather stood over her, a wrinkled hand pressed down on her shoulder. I crept toward them and sat near my mother. When she saw me, she smiled weakly.

"He'll be OK now," she said quietly. "He'll be OK."

But the next morning brought a nasty surprise.

Word had spread throughout Rokoya that Pa Osman Kamara, my grandfather, was harboring a man sick with smallpox. And they wanted him gone.

Shortly after sunrise, we heard a large group of people walking past my grandfather's house, headed toward the chief's compound. The entire village—men and women, young and old—had gathered together to demand our immediate departure from the village. As they walked, they shouted in Temene, making their anger and fear known to all.

"Death is here again!"

"Make them leave our village!"

"Let them go back to their own village!"

"No smallpox!"

"Chief, hear our cries and remember the deaths of our loved ones!"

My grandfather shook his head sadly, and a worried look crept over his lined, aging face.

"We had 300 people here in Rokoya just a year ago," he told us. "But then an outbreak of smallpox hit, and nearly a third of the village residents died in just a few months."

They wanted us gone. Every single one of them was terrified that Abu's infection would spread, taking the lives of their remaining loved ones.

Most of the residents of Rokoya were rice farmers, with a handful of fishermen and hunters mixed in. But on that day, none of them left the village to farm, fish, or hunt. They abandoned their duties without hesitation, driven by fear of the suffering that always accompanied smallpox. They were passionate in their protests. Loud, angry, and insistent. And although they didn't harass us directly, instead petitioning the chief, my mother and I could not help but feel afraid. We avoided windows, ducking behind my grandfather for protection any time we saw a villager passing by.

We had been so relieved just moments before. After a long and tedious journey, an emotional reunion with my grandfather, and the promise of healing from Bokari Nufu's expertise, we were plunged into panic and dismay.

"If I had known there had been such a deadly outbreak here in Rokoya, I would have stayed at home and tried harder to find medicine for Abu in Robomp Bana," my mother said, half to herself and half to me. "We never should have come."

At that moment, a woman passed by my grandfather's house on her way to join the protestors, shouting, "Smallpox took my only child!"

Following her was a teenaged boy who yelled, "It killed my older sister!"

The protest began early in the morning, and it was clear that people had come from all corners of Rokoya and even some surrounding villages to voice their disapproval. Soon a raucous crowd was gathered near the chief's home, and fairly soon afterwards it was clear the shouting and chanting had awakened the chief himself.

The villagers know that—regardless of their anger and mistrust—it was up to the chief to decide whether or not we should leave the village. When he awoke and heard the voices of the angry villagers, desperate to throw us out of their village, he acted quickly. He dispatched one of his men to run to my grandfather's house and tell him to come to the courthouse. The courthouse was just a shed with a bamboo roof in the front of the chief's house, but the entire community respected it as an official gathering place.

My grandfather was a respected elder at Rokoya village, one of the most honorable men in the village. He periodically gave advice and assistance to the chief on tricky decisions and helped settle disputes relating to land issues. The villagers called him "the great old man." But now his neighbors believed he had made a grave error by allowing his ill grandson into the village. And no matter his standing, he was subject to the chief's judgment.

My grandfather accompanied the chief's messenger back to the courthouse without protest. As close associates who respected each other, the two old men discussed the situation at length and compared ideas for how to resolve the protesting.

And the protesting continued. The chief and my grandfather stayed in the courthouse for nearly two hours, and the entire mob of angry villagers milled around outside in the baking sun the entire time.

Finally, the chief emerged, my grandfather trailing behind him. He held up both arms, and soon the yelling and talking quieted.

"The Great Old Man and I have reached a resolution," he boomed. "We have decided that his daughter and her sons will return to their own village to seek treatment for the elder son's smallpox. They will be gone by morning."

Hearing this, the villagers reluctantly began to leave the court area. In twos and threes, they headed back down the dirt roads toward their homes, discussing and gossiping as they went.

Once the majority of protesters had cleared away, my grandfather made his way back to his house and told us what the chief had said behind closed doors.

"He advised me to send you back home or quarantine you from Rokoya a mile or two into the woods," he told us, sneaking looks into the dark back room where Abu was resting. "I know it sounds harsh, but it's not a bad idea. And with smallpox, it's common to isolate the sick from the healthy."

My mother wrung her hands but nodded her head. She knew this was a plan that made sense, though she wasn't happy or comfortable with it.

"I think you should head to the woods," my grandfather continued. "That way, I'll be within reach if things get worse. You won't be far from help, even if we won't be together."

"Can we stay with you for the rest of today?" I piped up anxiously.

"Yes, Ansu. But we must keep quiet and out of sight. People are calm now, but they want you and your mother gone."

So we hunkered down, tended Abu through his fitful sleep, and waited.

On the morning of our third day in Rokoya, my grandfather and several of his friends headed two miles into the woods laden with palm leaves. They spent several hours building a simple hut using the leaves and large branches. That evening, my mother, my brother and I were escorted to the hut.

We did not know it at the time, but that hut would be our home for the next 33 days and nights.

Chapter 4

Life in Hiding

My family knew how to live simply. Everyone in my father's household knew how to make the most of a little, be frugal, and create workarounds when resources were scarce. We had lived through terrible harvests and years with no surplus to fall back on, and had managed to scrape by, smiling and optimistic for the future.

My family also knew how to live through crisis. Raging fires and torrential rains, fierce arguments and long-held grudges were all managed with patience and perseverance. We relied on each other for support when faced with catastrophe or tension, turning to our trusted little knot of beloved relatives when dismay flooded our hearts.

But my mother, Abu, and I found ourselves wholly unprepared for the mental and emotional stresses of isolation.

We were used to a loud, bustling life filled with voices, opinions, jokes, and helpful loved-ones elbowing their way into our personal space. Our large family was our sanctuary, and we all adored the safety and encouragement it provided. But confined to the tiny, hastily built hut my grandfather had erected to conceal us from the residents of Rokoya, silence hung heavy in the air.

And at times, that silence felt almost impossible to bear.

My mother seemed to be drowning in it herself, unable or unwilling to speak freely for fear of letting her sadness and worry spill out. I could see in her eyes that she was struggling, but she seldom spoke. When she did, it would sometimes be to reassure me in a harsh whisper.

"Stay strong, Ansu," she said. "We will get through this."

When we first moved into the hut, I expected my mother to be terrified, but she showed no signs of fear. It was hard to tell what was truly going on in her mind. She may have been crying internally, but outwardly she did her best to conceal her emotions. If her heart was beating faster, if she was worried and confused, or losing hope for my brother's recovery, I did not see it. Although she seemed somewhat tense, her exterior remained composed and quiet.

Looking back, I feel certain she was hiding her feelings for my sake. She knew that children react to what they see, that young people take their emotional cues from the adults around them. My mother knew that if she had been constantly screaming and broken down in tears, I might have become equally distraught. If my sick brother had tuned into her agitation and worry he, too, would have broken down and his condition might have worsened. So my mother acted as normally as she could. She stayed strong for me and for Abu.

I was wrestling with my own anxiety, but I did my best to master it. I was a young boy at the time, but mature for my age and able to think like an adult. I knew I needed to keep the peace that my mother was struggling to create. And that meant looking after Abu as he battled against the smallpox, but also supporting my mother as she struggled to navigate our situation.

The first few days in isolation were spent adjusting to our new surroundings. Our hut was built on high ground, atop a small hill with a broad, flat top. The slope had alternating patches of tall, stiff grass and smooth, green grass, but the clearing where our hut was situated was surrounded by a thick growth of trees with broad evergreen leaves. The front entrance faced the narrow trail road, while the back entrance was nearly covered by a big old cotton tree with enormous branches. The tree was so old that some of its roots had pushed through the ground and stretched out along the surface like gnarled fingers stretching toward something just out of reach.

The hut was on the outskirts of the village in a location that was difficult to reach. Coming from Rokoya, one would pass through a huge muddy swamp, full of wet, spongy terrain. Clusters of bamboo stalks and thick scrub plants peppered the swamp, making it even more challenging to navigate. After crossing the swamp, thick growths of palm and cotton trees sprung up, shielding our hut from curious eyes. My grandfather chose this location strategically, considering both the reasons we needed to be isolated and the importance of making access to us challenging and discouraging. He wanted his fellow villagers to believe we were long gone, so he tucked us out of sight in a spot that was far off the beaten path.

Except for the wind blowing and birds singing during the day, the area where the hut was built was very quiet.

Under other circumstances, the silence would have been relaxing. But with Abu suffering from smallpox and my mother trapped in stony silence, the stillness felt oppressive.

A cherished break came in the form of my grandfather's visits. He would come to check on us every day around midday, bringing food, water, and much-needed conversation. The healer Bokari Nufu made daily stops to treat my brother and check on his progress, and a few members of my grandfather's household stopped by on occasion. But my grandfather's visits were what kept us sane.

"Well, how are my brave ones doing today?" he'd ask as he wrapped my little body in his sinewy arms. Then he'd look down at me with a sad smile and squeeze my shoulder before heading back to visit Abu with my mother.

He would sit on the hard, dusty ground near my brother's frail form, and speak quietly with him for a few minutes. Abu's strength was slowly returning as Bokari Nufu's remedies took hold, but he was still frail and prone to exhaustion.

"Do not tire yourself, Abu," my grandfather would say. "I'll be back again tomorrow, and you can update me then."

Then he would eat the midday meal with us, bringing reports and gossip from the village and doing his best to distract us. I tried to delay his departure—asking ridiculous and detailed questions to keep him talking—but he had his own duties to attend to, and never stayed more than an hour.

"I'm sorry, Ansu, but I must go," he told me, sounding regretful and weary. "Try not to get into too much trouble before I come back tomorrow, OK?"

I would promise with a weak smile, then stand and watch his retreating back from the front door of our hut.

If the days were long and dull, the nights were long and miserable.

We never had visitors at night throughout the thirty-three days we stayed in the woods. When the sun went down, it was just the three of us and the surrounding wildlife. We could hear animals rustling about in the trees, never visible but always present. My mother and I did our best to be brave and calm, but there is something decidedly sinister about hearing a wild animal going about its business just outside your home. Knowing that it can see you, though you cannot see it.

My mother sometimes told me stories to distract me from our situation, spinning tales of adventure or humor in her low whisper while she held me in her lap.

"Ansu, did you know that faith can move a mountain?" she asked me one night. She was still on high alert, listening to Abu's restlessness just a few feet away, but also doing her best to comfort me. And herself.

"Before you were born," she continued, "my first child, your older sister, Fatmata, became very sick with cholera. At first we were hopeful, but instead of improving, she just got worse and worse. At one point, she was so sick that the healer from our village said she only had a few weeks to live. But with our faith and prayers, our love and care, she beat the cholera. And now she's perfectly well and makes trouble back at home!"

She chuckled softly and drew me closer.

"Just have faith," she said. "Abu will make it through this and soon we will be on our way back to Robomp Bana."

I had not known that my strong-willed sister, Fatmata, had ever been ill, and learning that she had pulled through brought me such relief. If she could beat back cholera, surely Abu would do the same with smallpox.

These stories became our nightly ritual, something we did to calm down and unwind after long, tense days. One night she was in the middle of a story about her own childhood when the light on our pan lamp suddenly cut off. It was our only light source and had run out of kerosene. We sat for a moment in the thick darkness, barely able to see a foot in front of our faces.

"Well," my mother said quietly, "I guess that means it's time to sleep!"

That night, we slept in a darkness so complete it felt like a blanket wrapped around us.

But nights weren't always dark and peaceful. Many were dark and restless.

My brother did not do well at night. His pain and suffering seemed to worsen when the sun set, and my mother and I had to stay vigilant. The smallpox made him delirious, and in this altered state he would often leave the hut at night and wander around in the woods. As he walked, he had long rambling conversations as if there were other people around him, though he stumbled through the trees entirely on his own. As soon as we realized he was missing, my mother and I would spring into action, heading into the woods to track him down. Deep in his delusions, he never wanted to be found and would hide behind trees to avoid us. His pain drove him to act in this bizarre and disoriented way, and I could tell it was all my mother could do to remain calm as she watched her son staggering through the darkness having imaginary conversations. It sometimes took several hours to find him and walk him back to the safety of the hut.

"What if we don't realize he's gone one night and he makes it into Rokoya?" I asked my mother after a particularly long and trying search for Abu.

"He won't. He never gets that far."

But she didn't sound convinced. And I realized I had planted a brand new worry in her overworked mind.

Despite all that was happening—despite every sleepless night and frustrating setback—my faith remained strong. I knew in my heart that my brother would survive and prayed for him silently as I laid on the hard floor each night. I knew that our exile in the woods was Abu's last and only chance at recovery, and I clung to my belief that he was strong enough to pull through. I couldn't imagine losing my older brother to smallpox. I knew that our desperate situation, uncomfortable living quarters, and numerous stresses did not matter. What mattered was Abu's life.

The first two weeks of our voluntary exile were the hardest. On top of the tense isolation and Abu's nightly escape attempts, we dealt with non-stop tsetse fly bites during the day and relentless mosquito bites at night. The weather seemed determined to punish us, too. It was in the beginning of September when my brother first came down with smallpox, which meant the rainy season was almost over, but we still got the occasional downpour. One afternoon during our second week in the hut, the clouds kept the sky dark and gloomy all day, and by nightfall a heavy rain began to fall. The thunder shook our tiny hut and the lightning tormented poor Abu. As the night wore on, the rain became so severe that water surged through the hastily made roof of our hut and soaked us to the bone. That was a long and trying night.

"Well," I said to my mother as we huddled together trying to find a spot under the roof that *wasn't* leaking, "at least it's too wet for the mosquitoes to be out tonight."

She smiled broadly at my joke and drew me closer.

By day twenty, we finally saw some signs of real improvement in my brother's condition. He began to rest better and slept longer at night, finally abandoning his delirious walks in the dark forest. The blisters on his body began to burst and pus drained out, which meant the disease was beginning to leave his system.

Bokari Nufu, the healer, began coming more frequently once he saw that Abu was moving steadily toward wellness. In fact, sometimes he stayed with us all day. On the days he spent in the hut with Abu, he constantly rubbed the ground ashes of a root all over my brother's body. Abu's entire skin was pulled tighter as the medicine dried out, which helped to drain the pus seeping out of the blisters. It did not look like a pleasant process, but Abu was patient and good-natured, so he bore it as best he could. Mostly in silence.

As my brother continued to improve day after day, he started speaking up more and became aware of his surroundings. Living through smallpox had been like living through a long, muddled, confusing dream. And Abu was finally waking up. When he had enough of a grasp on his situation to ask, "Why are we here?", we knew he had made it through the worst of the disease. As he asked more questions it became clear that he had no knowledge of how or when he contracted smallpox and no memory of the long journey we'd taken to arrive in this tiny hut on my grandfather's lands. Mother told him she would explain everything to him later when his condition was better, and we were back in our village. Abu was healing but still weak and did not press for more information.

All we wanted was his speedy recovery, and finally, it came faster and more continuously. Abu's eyes regained some of their clarity, and he began to regain his strength. Toward the end of our third week, he became restless enough to get out of bed and explore our surroundings. That day, I walked him around the hut. The next day, he was strong enough to walk on his own. The day after that, he even left the hut to amble among the trees.

In the days that followed, as he inched toward a full recovery, my brother began spending time under the big old cotton tree located at the back entrance of the hut. He would sit on the exposed roots to relax and nap, though sometimes he'd softly call me out to sit near him.

"Ansu," he'd rasp. "Come keep me company, won't you?"

I would scamper out to join him as fast my skinny legs would take me. He'd been so silent during the worst of his illness, but the closer he came to recovery, the more talkative he became. And despite our strange and stressful circumstances, I loved those long afternoons trading stories with my big brother. I wondered if I would ever have the opportunity to spend this much lazy, quiet time with him again, and soaked it all up just in case.

"Tell me a story from the Quran," he'd say. "You have such a great memory, I know you know them all!"

When we were out there at the tree, our mother would sit at a distance and watch us talking. Abu and I had always been close, and she could see we were becoming even closer. I idolized him for his standing in our family and community, and he admired me for my ability to learn and read, and memorize.

"You're such a smart boy," he told me, mussing my hair with one of his huge, dry hands. "I really don't know how you do it. Father teaches us verses from the Quran one day, and you're able to recite every word in Arabic the next day. Such a mind you have!"

I was too shy to say so, but I was thinking how much I admired him. I had always envisioned myself following in my older brother's footsteps by becoming a successful farmer who grew enormous crops and was essential to his village community.

So imagine my surprise when one day, as we were seated under the tree, my brother mentioned the word "school."

"None of us have English education," he said. "If Mom and Dad decided to send you to school in Freetown, it wouldn't be a bad idea."

"Why me?" I asked.

"Why you? You know the answer to that, Ansu," he said gently, looking down at me with smiling eyes. "Your brain is as sharp as a knife. I know that you could learn from English books and retain what you learned as you do with the Quran, even at your young age. There is no doubt you could finish school and do well there. Don't you want to learn?"

"I do," I said, but was quiet afterwards. He had given me much to consider.

Respect for the elders and putting the elders first in everything is very important in both African and Muslim traditions. The norms of due respect in our culture dictated that if any of us children were to go to school, Abu would have been the first. But clearly, he was passing that honor along to me and seeing how I reacted.

Those discussions under the cotton tree planted seeds in my mind that would one day blossom into reality. But that time was a long way off.

Back at the hut, Abu continued to recover day by day and night by night. Soon all three of us began to look forward to the much-anticipated day when we could leave the woods and go back to our own village. Although we were eager to get back home, Mother and I both agreed that the day of our departure would be determined by my brother's condition. Although our time living in the wilderness had been nerve-wracking and awful, we were prepared to stay there as long as it took for my brother to fully recover. To leave prematurely and weaken him was out of the question.

My mother was also acutely aware that—with the exception of my grandfather's household—the residents of Rokoya believed we were long gone. On the day of protest when the Chief announced that he had reached an agreement with my grandfather, the villagers believed we had left their village and gone back to where we came from. Since the hearts and minds of the Rokoya population were still grieving and smallpox was still a burning subject, my mother understood that it would have been a grave mistake to be seen by any of the villagers.

The timing of our departure had to be just right and we scraped up our last bits of patience to wait for its arrival.

Thankfully, just as suddenly as the smallpox disease had entered my brother's body, so it departed. Every day he felt better and stronger than the previous one, and he never had any bad days or setbacks once he started to improve. In fact, after a full month in the tiny hut he was feeling so good that he became anxious to leave the woods and go back to our village.

"I'm telling you, Mother, I am ready!" he pleaded.

"I know you feel ready, Abu, but we must be cautious," she soothed.

Both of us encouraged him to slow down until we were sure he was completely free of the disease. He did his best to understand, but now that he was lucid and active and aware of how long we'd been away from home, he became impatient and wanted to leave.

And after a few days of pleading and insisting he was ready, Mother gave in.

"Well, I said that the day we left the woods would be determined by Abu's condition," she said. "Since his current condition is 'well enough to pester his mother every five minutes about going home', I'm going to conclude that it's time to go."

Abu smiled and closed his eyes. "Thank you, Mother," he said. "I know I am ready."

So that morning, we began preparing to leave the hut that had been our home for thirty-three days and nights.

When my grandfather arrived at midday as usual, bringing food and water for our meal, he immediately saw that our bags were packed.

"Yabu, is it time?" he asked. "Oh, Abu, are you finally well? I cannot believe it!"

He dropped the provisions to the ground and stretched out his arms. Happy tears filled his eyes as he gathered the three of us up and drew us to him. He had greeted us with tears of sadness and distress upon our arrival, and he was seeing us off with tears of joy.

But before we left for good, we had to do one last thing.

When smallpox ravaged the country of Sierra Leone during the 1950s and '60s, many people held on to a traditional belief about how to deal with the place of quarantine. If a person suffering from smallpox is isolated in a shelter outside his or her village and dies in the shelter, he or she should be buried in that shelter. If the person survives, the shelter must be set on fire along with everything that was in it during the period of the illness. People believed that taking any items out of the quarantine shelter is like taking the disease along with them.

To carry out this tradition, my mother, Abu, and I had to exit our hut with only the clothes we were wearing. The few pieces of extra clothing and all of mother's personal items had to be left behind, as well as her spare pair of shoes. I owned no shoes, instead walked barefooted like all the boys in our village, so I left no shoes behind. But I did sacrifice one extra rappel, a long cloth that covered the upper and lower part of the body. Abu left the few extra items of clothing he'd brought along, too. It wasn't much, but it still felt strange to abandon every object we'd used for the past month and walk free of the hut entirely unencumbered.

We stayed in our hut for one more night. Early the next morning, my grandfather returned with a few of his men carrying dry grass, branches, and dry leaves. Carefully, they piled this kindling in the center of the hut and lit a flame with matches. Since the hut had been built more than a month ago using mostly palm leaves, it was quite dry and caught fire quickly and easily. We all watched solemnly as it burned to the ground.

"Be careful and take your time," my grandfather said as he embraced my mother. "I will be thinking of you as you journey home."

"Thank you for everything, Father," Mother said through her tears. "We would never have made it without your help."

"It was nothing. I am so glad you are all well, though I will miss you terribly!"

We each embraced him, and thanked him, and cried with him. Then we turned toward home and began the long walk back to Robomp Bana.

The two-day trip to Rokoya had seemed never-ending but the journey home was much shorter. We passed through Rokoya without being noticed, since everyone in the village was out tending their farms and away from their houses during the daytime. All was quiet. Abu was well again, so we barely needed to stop at all to let him rest, and covered ground more quickly. In fact, we left Rokoya in the early morning and by late afternoon of the same day we had arrived home in our village.

"We are back!" my mother sang as she poked her head into our home's kitchen.

My sisters immediately began shouting and squealing and rushing to embrace us. My brothers were on their way back from the fields, and later told us they could hear the ruckus from far in the distance. They soon joined our tearful and raucous reunion.

Once the excitement had died down a bit, Abu asked about our father.

"He is resting," my sister Marie said. "Go and see him!" she urged, shoving Abu toward the bedroom.

I did not accompany Abu in to see our father but could hear the murmured cries of excitement and relief from the other room. And a few moments later when Abu emerged, he looked exhausted but happy. He smiled knowingly at me, and I smiled back.

The news of our return spread quickly, and awakened our village in joy. That night the villagers gathered around our house to celebrate our return. The reason for the gathering was twofold: The first was the excitement that my brother survived his battle with smallpox. The second was because of who we were in our village. My father, being the religious head of the village, was highly respected by all and his children were cared for and well-known in the village. It was a celebration of thankfulness to God for giving my brother a second chance at life.

The gathering was unplanned, but word spread quickly that we had returned, and Abu was healthy once more, so a large group of neighbors began gathering around the front of our mud house to welcome us home. Laughing and talking was soon mixed with drum beats and women's voices singing Temene songs.

After resting and relaxing for a few days, Abu insisted on picking up where he left off. He soon started his daily trips back to the farm and resumed his usual activities, taking his place as the head of the household once more. He returned quickly to his old life, but the memory of his battle with smallpox lingered. As did the scars that covered his body and face, eternal reminders of the month he spent fighting for his life in a hut in the woods.

Abu's return brought light and joy back to our household. We were once again a united, happy family who not only believed in each other but also that our older brother would continue to lead the family to many successful harvest seasons to come.

Chapter 5

A New Life Path

Abu's struggle with smallpox and our month in hiding had been tense, trying, and frightening. So I was relieved to have returned to the easy rhythms of life in Robomp Bana. It felt good to slip back into old roles and perform familiar tasks. I even welcomed the endless teasing of my sisters and enjoyed the hard labor of field work. It was good to be home and be myself again.

But I could tell that something was shifting within my family. The conversation that Abu and I had under the cotton tree was lingering in his mind, and I could tell he had started to discuss the subject with our parents. And that it was weighing on them all.

In the 1950s in the smaller villages of Sierra Leone, most families felt that education was a very low priority. They saw their male children as future farmers—ones who would likely take over responsibility for the family land when they came of age—and female children as future wives and mothers. School was expensive, did not provide the skills and temperament village children needed to be successful and happy in life, and felt incredibly impractical to most parents.

Like most of their peers, my parents were not naturally inclined to send any of us to school. But Abu had become stuck on the idea. He felt so strongly that I would benefit from a formal education that he basically started campaigning on my behalf with our dad. He spent nearly two months having secret, earnest conversations with our dad, trying his best to convince him that schooling in Freetown was something I deserved and needed. He worked on our mother, too, though she was a bit more flexible. Her stance was that she wanted whatever was best for her children, and if that meant school, so be it. She would've preferred that we stay together as a family, but truly had our best interests at heart…and knew that I was unusually intelligent and a great candidate for academics. If our dad would concede, so would she.

So Abu concentrated on Dad.

And Dad was not easily convinced. He was reluctant to let one of his children leave home, leave the farm for school where everything was theoretical instead of practical. But Abu continued to press him.

"We'll hardly feel the absence of just one family member," Abu said. "One less worker wouldn't have a real impact on the farm's prosperity. As long as I'm healthy and strong, you'll have me to run things. And with the help and support of our neighbors, we'll get everything done right on time."

"How can you be sure?" my father asked. "How can you know it will be so?"

"I cannot predict the future," Abu said. "But I can promise you that if I need to work twice as hard to make up for Ansu's absence, I'll do it."

Our father wrestled with the idea for many weeks, weighing the pros and cons and worrying endlessly about sending me away. But Abu was relentless, and finally wore him down. He resigned himself to giving one of his sons the chance to have a formal education.

Abu had made it clear that I was the natural choice to send to school, but even if Dad had been forced to choose one of us entirely on his own, it likely would've been me. He had watched me as he taught us all the Quran, had seen how talented I was and my natural aptitude for learning. I was the natural choice, and he knew that meant letting me go.

When the day came to announce to the whole family that I would be leaving, he called me into his room.

"Ansu, I need to talk to you, just the two of us," he told me.

"OK," I said, feeling wary. "Is everything OK?"

"Yes, of course," he said. "But some things in your life are about to change, and I want to discuss them with you. Did Abu speak with you about going to school while he was recovering from his illness?"

"Yes, Sir."

"Well, he's been speaking with me and your mother about it, too. For several months now. He believes very strongly that you should get a formal education that you would thrive if given the chance to go to school. I would rather have you home, of course," he said with a smile, "but Abu has convinced me to send you to Freetown. Do you know why?"

"Why?"

"Well, you have always amazed me with your ability to memorize Quran verses, and you do it so much faster than any of your brothers or sisters. And although we will miss you very much, I believe you will make us very proud. I will hold my head high knowing that my smart, brave young son has gotten a full education."

His voice was full of emotion as he spoke. He reached out and placed a hand on my small shoulder.

"Would you like to try it, Ansu?" he asked. "Do you want to go to school in Freetown and learn English and math and other subjects?"

I felt overwhelmed and numb. The idea of leaving home for good made my brain feel cloudy. I loved studying the Quran and the prospect of learning other subjects appealed to me, but I felt frozen. Unable to make a solid decision.

"I will do whatever you and Mom think is best," I finally replied.

He looked at me for a long moment. I was so honored to be the one chosen, singled out for formal education, but the thought of leaving my loved ones made me feel small and afraid.

"Well, I've given your brother my word. And he's certainly convinced that you'll do extraordinarily well at school. So if you are really willing to trust our opinion, I think we'll make this happen for you," he said. "I'm going to announce my decision at family gathering night tonight. Then tomorrow I'll send a message to your older sister, Fatmata, in Freetown asking her to come back home for a family discussion."

"OK, Sir," I said, a little dizzy.

"Until we all gather, please don't mention this to anyone else," he told me.

I nodded. He squeezed my shoulder and sent me out. I wandered through our house in a daze, finally making my way to the back where I sat beneath my favorite tree and tried to make sense of my whirlwind of feelings.

Before I knew it, it was time for the family gathering. Everyone assembled before the fire, talking and laughing, until my father stood up to speak.

"Yabu and I, along with our eldest son, Abu, have decided to let one of our younger children join Fatmata in Freetown where he will enroll in school," he said. "We have come to the unanimous decision that Ansu is ready for this great challenge."

The talking and laughing had vanished. The entire community had become quite somber, and it was so quiet you could hear the faintest breeze rustling the leaves of the trees.

I looked out on all those expectant faces with mixed emotions. I knew I was about to go on an amazing adventure, begin a new chapter in my life, but I would miss my siblings and family so very much.

I saw my maternal grandmother, who had been with us for three months, who had stayed with our family while Mom and I took Abu to Rokoya to recover. I could tell she was holding back tears. She was just recovering from the mental and emotional strain of Abu's battle with smallpox, and now another of her grandchildren would leave the village permanently? She tried to smile at me, but I could tell that the news was hard for her to bear.

But despite our sadness, Dad kept his promise and followed his plan. He sent word to Fatmata and a few days after receiving his message, she and her husband arrived in Robomp Bana. Dad welcomed them both heartily, and Mom worked hard to prepare a feast to share with the entire family.

Fatmata helped Mom get the food ready while her husband, a man named Sorie Ibrahim Mansaray, chatted with Dad.

"Something is wrong," I heard her say to my sister Isatu. But Isatu just shook her head and focused on the cooking. Fatmata looked around her at all the women working quietly, taking in their sullen expressions and furrowing her brow. She knew something was wrong, but no one would explain. She let out a sigh and focused on her tasks. She must've known we were holding our tongues out of respect to our parents, our elders, and that she'd be told in time.

"Abu certainly looks happier than the rest of you," she said under her breath. "Maybe this family news is about him."

It wasn't until after we'd eaten that she finally learned what was affecting us all.

Once everything was cleaned up from the meal, Dad gathered us all again. He broke the news to them that he and Mom had decided it was in the best interests of our whole family to send me to Freetown to join her and attend school there.

"Oh, thank goodness!" Fatmata exclaimed. "All your frowns and sour moods had me thinking it was something MUCH worse. We'd love to have Ansu come live with us, of course."

"We actually have a group of boys from my side of the family living with us now," her husband, Sorie, added. "They're all in school, too, and we'd love to have you join them."

They promised to take good care of me and make sure I got the best education possible. I could feel a tiny wave of relief passing over my family members, though they were still solemn.

As for me, I was still grappling with a flood of emotions. Although I mostly thought about how this enormous change would affect me, I thought, too, about my parents. I knew beyond any doubt that this had been a very difficult decision for them to make. Both of them had grown up on farms, in environments where farming was not only their primary activity but their way of life. And in our village, farming was the activity that sons and daughters, young and old, dreamed of and engaged in on a day-by-day and season-by-season basis. They had been immersed in farming their whole lives, and in teaching their children—myself included—how to keep the land healthy and the crops growing. To imagine a different future for me must have felt foreign and bizarre to them.

I thought back to being a tiny boy, before I could be much help in the fields. Back then, I spent my days chasing away the birds so they wouldn't eat our seedlings. I loved doing this and it had felt like play, but I realized as I combed over my memories that it had been my job. My assignment. My mother had told me to do this, to keep the birds clear of the freshly planted fields. I was learning to be a good farmer before I even understood what a farmer did.

But the decision was made, and my path was changing.

Fatmata and her husband decided to stay with our family for two more days to prepare me for the journey to Freetown. During that time, my mother took the few pieces of clothing I had down to the river side to wash them. I did not have a suitcase or bag, so my sister Marie gave me a pillowcase to stuff my clothes into. I had little else to take with me; No books or shoes, no real belongings of my own. Just a few modest garments and my eagerness to learn.

Once I was packed, I began the process of saying goodbye to my friends in the village. Like me, they felt a mix of excitement for my new life and sadness at losing my presence in their own lives. I was hugged more times than I can count, given blessings, and told to remember the loved ones I was leaving behind. It was emotionally overwhelming, but I felt cherished and supported.

The night before we were to depart, my father recited some special prayers for me at evening prayers at the mosque. The entire congregation wished me good luck, and their warmth buoyed me. I was so nervous that night, and hearing their voices helped me feel less afraid.

I spent some time with my maternal grandmother that night, too. She was 88 and starting to show her age, and also very reluctant to let me go. I was one of her favorites, and she actually campaigned for someone else among my brothers and sisters to be selected for schooling in Freetown because she did not want us to be separated. I tried to soothe her, saying I'd be back to visit and see her. (Little did I know it was to be a final separation; shortly after I left the village, she became ill and died.)

The next morning, my family, friends, and neighbors came to the wharf to see me off. Around 10 a.m., the passenger boat for Freetown arrived and Fatmata, her husband, and I climbed aboard. As the boat pulled away and I waved to everyone gathered at the wharf, I felt a heavy weight on my chest. The landscape I'd known my whole life, the people who'd loved and raised me were getting smaller and smaller as the boat moved further from shore. I was going to a city I'd never visited before at the age of 10 and had no idea what to expect. I'd spent my life among houses made of dirt, palm leaves, and bamboo. What would Freetown be like? Certainly not the quiet, natural, routine-reliant life I'd been used to.

Fatmata saw my furrowed brow and pulled me into her skirts for a hug.

"I know you're scared, Ansu," she said. "But we're here to help you. You'll never be alone."

I nodded but felt a hot tear streak down my face.

Was I truly ready for this?

I was about to find out.

Chapter 6

So Much to Learn

We docked at the J-Net Terminal in Freetown around 5 p.m. that evening, stepping off the boat and immediately walking a block away to a taxi stand. Fatmata hustled me into the rickety car which sped us all toward the eastern part of Freetown where she, her husband, and the other school-aged boys all lived. My head was full of the sights and sounds of the bustling city, and I gaped out the taxi window as the buildings, bikes, people, streets, animals, and other cars flew by. I had never been in a car before, and the sensation was a little dizzying!

About 15 minutes later, we arrived. Fatmata and her husband had built several rooms behind their house, which they rented to tenants. Their entire compound was fenced all around and was crowded with people. Since I was used to living in a home with lots of loud, raucous family members, it felt comfortable to be among all these people at Fatmata's home.

There were eight school-aged boys, including myself, who lived under the care and guardianship of my sister and her husband. I was among the three youngest at 10 years old, with a 9-year-old and 11-year-old who were close to me in age. Two boys aged 15 and 16 were in the middle, and the oldest ones were 18 and 19. They were mostly cousins from both sides of the family who had been brought from various parts of the country by their parents to attend school in Freetown. Within a few days of my arrival, I understood that these boys were part of my family now. Regardless of what part of Sierra Leone any of us came from or how we were related, in that household we were brought up to look after each other and regard each other as brothers.

My very first night there, one of the older boys, Sheka Mansaray, took me aside.

"Ansu, listen," he said. "You are one of us now, and that means we will always help you. You should know, too, that your sister expects us to protect one another and live in harmony and peace at all times."

He paused and I nodded silently.

"That doesn't mean we can't have any fun," he said, noting the worry in my face. "Teasing, pranks, all that stuff is no big deal. But no fighting. And if someone needs help, you must always be willing to help. Does that make sense?"

"Yes. Thank you, Sheka."

He thumped me on the back and headed off into the house. It was an oddly formal little speech, but it gave me comfort. I knew I would be safe and taken care of here, and that was a huge relief.

School was not yet in session when I arrived but would begin one month later. I was glad to have this time to adjust to my new life without the additional stress of acclimating to school and studying. Sheka and Wusu Sankoh, the two oldest boys, took me under their wings and organized a few "get to know Freetown" trips so I could become familiar with my new home.

The very first time we went out, we visited Hope Day Elementary School, where I would eventually study. It was just a few blocks from the house, so it was a short walk and Sheka and Wusu knew that Fatmata had her eye on this school for me. Two of the other boys were already enrolled there, and that would enable me to have companions on my walk to school and friends to help me get used to being a student. We walked around the perimeter of the long, brick, single-floor building with its tin roof. I peered into the windows to see that there were several separated classrooms inside. There was also a smaller building set apart from the classrooms where the administrators had their offices. I ran my hands over the brick walls, daydreaming about my life as a student there.

Our next stop was the nearby soccer stadium where most of the boys played after school and on the weekends.

"Do you play soccer, Ansu?" Wusu asked.

"I don't know how," I said.

"Well, you'll have to learn!" Sheka laughed.

They made sure to give me a few quick tutorials before the school year began. Soccer is a must for all Sierra Leone schoolboys.

A few days later, Sheka and Wusu took me to the historic King Jimmy Market, a massive trading center within Freetown's city limits that is situated on the river. Traders from towns both near and far arrived at the market with their goods to sell. There was so much to see, and I was lucky to have two protective and knowledgeable guides. Sheka and Wusu kept a close eye on me as we explored

King Jimmy Market, touching and staring, though never buying.

Back at Fatmata's house, there was only one bedroom allocated for the eight of us, and only one bed! Sheka was the oldest boy among us and Wusu was the second oldest, so the two of them got to sleep on the bed. The rest of us spread our mats on the floor of the living room. We all shared the bedroom during the day for changing clothes and other things, but at night the room was only for the oldest boys.

I was only 10 years old at the time and tended to be quiet and a little bashful around new people. I mostly kept to myself until I'd become acquainted with strangers or new friends. But the people I lived with in my sister's house were family, and family was different. I was quite comfortable and talkative around my brothers and sisters, and soon felt the same level of comfort around my cousins. Fatmata's husband was a devout Muslim and his faith guided him to treat everyone in his household with kindness and compassion. He constantly reminded me and the other boys to live in peace, unity, and brotherhood. And we did; it was easy to feel accepted and relaxed among such happy, serene family members.

After a few weeks had passed, Fatmata began the preparations for me to start school. She registered me at Hope Day, the school I'd scouted with Sheka and Wusu a few weeks previously. About a week before the school opened for the academic year, my sister and her husband took me to the school to register and pay our fees. I was glad to have visited with Sheka and Wusu a few weeks before, but still felt tiny and overwhelmed signing up for classes at the administrative building. Once registration was taken care of, we went to Kissy Road Market to purchase school supplies, a uniform, and a pair of shoes.

Freetown is divided into three main areas; eastern, central, and western. All three had shopping areas called "marketplaces" where goods of all kinds are sold in open stands, tables, booths, and small stores. The markets are always packed with people, but on Saturdays they're bustling and overcrowded since it is the busiest shopping day of the week. People of all ages gathered there, alone or with parents, relatives, or friends. It was a social hub where everyone met to socialize and run errands.

Kissy Road Market was smaller than King Jimmy, but just as bustling. As we wove in between the stalls and booths, I saw people from all 16 ethnic tribes of Sierra Leone shopping and chatting with shopkeepers. As we passed by the section of the market where seafood was sold, a strong salty, fishy smell floated by, causing me to wrinkle my nose. But as we moved on toward the household wares and clothing, the stench dissipated.

"Are all of these people here every day, selling?" I asked my sister.

"Some are, some aren't," she explained. "Anyone who wants to sell their goods in this market can do so any day. They just need to show up and set up their stall or shop. Someone from the city council called a 'collector' will walk around in the morning to collect a daily fee from each trader. The trader gets a receipt to prove he's paid for the day and can go about his business."

I loved the idea of a market where anyone could sell, and a different group of goods would be available to shoppers every single day.

Getting new clothes for my new life felt momentous, and even though the clothes themselves were fairly boring, I loved them. I loved how they felt on my body and what they represented: An exciting new era for me.

All students in Sierra Leone—primary and secondary, private and public—were required to wear a uniform. No exceptions, no excuses! The uniforms were color coded to indicate academic level and school attended. Girls always had a uniform that included a skirt or dress. Boys attending school in the lower grades wore shorts and button-front shirts, and at higher grades they switched to long pants. My own uniform was a khaki shirt and khaki shorts, and I treasured them.

The shoes, on the other hand, posed a problem.

I had spent the first ten years of my life walking barefoot around my home, the farm, and my village and had never become accustomed to wearing shoes. The pair Fatmata bought for me were black lace-up sneakers, and I knew they were handsome, but they felt so strange on my feet. Everyone around me seemed to have mastered the art of walking in shoes, but I felt like a newborn calf who couldn't get its footing. I tried to practice wearing them and walking around my bedroom, but still felt uncoordinated and awkward. *Would I trip over my own feet on my first day at school? Would the other students laugh at me?*

I fretted over those shoes night after night. And the nights sped by until I found myself staring at my bedroom ceiling on the night before my first day of school. My stomach was in knots and my mind full. I could hardly tell if I was more excited or worried. But before I could decide for sure, the sun rose and it was time to get ready.

Words cannot fully describe everything I felt that day. I was overcome by emotions: happiness, nervousness, bashfulness, and intimidation. As I clomped through the front doors, awkward in my new shoes and sweating through my uniform, I felt fear clamp down on my heart. The halls were teeming with other students, talking and teasing and walking confidently to their classes. I had my two cousins from Fatmata's house to rely on, but still felt nervous and overwhelmed.

My two fellow schoolmates had warned me that, as a newcomer, I could expect initiation, some form of cruel behavior from the other boys at Hope Day School that most new students dealt with at the beginning of the school year. Some examples of initiation pranks were hit and run, confiscating books and pens, or even stealing one's lunch. It was habitual for the boys and girls in the higher classes to "welcome" a newcomer by making him or her miserable and terrified on the first day of school. For no apparent reason, some of the older boys and girls took advantage of the younger students just for the fun of it. Boys did it to boys and girls to girls.

I was lucky, though, since I had two experienced Hope Day School students to protect me from this bullying. They promised to keep an eye on me, and were as good as their word.

They helped me find my classroom, and as I settled into my chair, I kept my eyes down. I didn't want to make eye contact with anyone, catch anyone's attention or interest.

All I wanted was to blend in, seem normal, and fade into the background. I was terrified that someone would ask me a question, and that the question would be in English. All I spoke was my native Temene language, but I didn't want anyone to know that. I was surrounded by strange boys and girls who might reveal my secret with one simple question, and the thought kept me rigid with fear.

I did allow my eyes to dart around the room a little to take in my surroundings. The classroom was a medium-sized square room with white walls, a huge chalkboard at the front, and two large windows at the back. The other students around me were chatting and laughing at their desks, the room buzzing with noise until our teacher arrived.

Mrs. Turner was a slightly chubby woman who wore large glasses with thick, clunky lenses. As she padded into the room holding books and papers, the chatting quickly subsided.

The first order of the day was mandatory roll call to ensure everyone listed on the class register logbook was present. When my name was called, it was unclear to me whether I should answer "Na" which means "Yes" in Temene, or just say nothing. The other students were responding in Krio, so I was unsure what I should do.

"Ansu Kamara?"

At first, I was silent but the teacher kept on calling my name and also looked directly at me.

"Ansu Kamara?"

When the name of the Krio boy seated in front of me was called, I noticed he just raised his right hand and the teacher skipped him and called another name.

"Ansu Kamara?!?"

My heart was thundering inside my chest. When Mrs. Turner continued to call my name, louder and more insistently each time, I thought for a minute then raised my right hand.

She skipped me and called another name.

I let out a long, silent sigh of relief.

That interaction with my teacher taught me the very first thing I learned at my new school: Observe and react. I used this newfound knowledge for the rest of that first day, and it served me well. If the class stood up, I stood up with them. If they seated themselves again, I also sat down. I assumed any movement in the classroom was in reaction to a direct instruction by the teacher because each time her lips moved, the class did something. I did not understand what she was saying in English, but I noticed that whenever her lips moved, the class did something. I figured I would deal with learning the words later. Right now, I just had to stay out of trouble.

Speaking of trouble, I did make some exceptions to my rule of "do what everyone around you is doing." When the other students started talking across the class or throwing books at each other, I remained calm and sat still. For one thing, the teacher's lips were not moving when the kids began acting out. For another thing, I knew what misbehaving looked like and wasn't about to push my luck!

The first day of school for students in Sierra Leone is more like orientation than regular class, so I spent much of the day getting to know Mrs. Turner and being introduced to the format my lessons would take. I learned about outdoor class, a tradition that was common in elementary schools; once a week, the teacher would take the entire class outdoors to sit on the recess benches for an hour of general discussion. I would come to love this practice eventually, but on the first day I was too terrified to participate at all.

In fact, I was so nervous and worried that first day that I sat at the very back of the class and did my best to keep quiet. At recess, my two housemates from Fatmata's protected me from any potential bullies. As I stood, nervously sandwiched between them, they assured me that if I made it through this first day without incident, the rest of the year would be problem-free, too. That was somewhat reassuring to hear, but back in the classroom I felt vulnerable again. I was unsure of my language skills and felt completely out of place. I tried not to attract attention from the teacher or other students, and counted the minutes until I could go back home.

Once the final bell rang in the late afternoon, my sister came by the school to walk me and the other two boys back home. I was so relieved to see her.

"How did it go today?" Fatmata asked.

"I don't know. It was fine, I suppose," I mumbled.

She smiled a small smile and patted me on the back, somehow sensing that she shouldn't press me for more details. The four of us walked back home quietly.

The other five boys who lived with me at Fatmata's attended different schools in Freetown. When that first school day was finally over and I returned home, I felt so relieved to be back among the boys I'd already gotten to know. We ate our meal together, and then everyone began working on whatever housework they had been assigned. We sat together in groups to do our studies. We assisted each other with our school homework and with our daily studies. I had no homework from my first day but sat with them as they worked.

I slept soundly that night, exhausted from all I'd seen and done and discovered. To be perfectly honest, that first day of school had been miserable. I was so grateful to have the opportunity to go and learn, but seeing and being among so many strange and unfriendly boys and girls had worn me out.

My second day of school was slightly different and not quite as stressful. I was able to relax a little that day after I found out the classroom was comprised of diverse groups of boys and girls from different ethnic and tribal backgrounds and that I was not the only Temene boy in the classroom. Some of the other tribes represented were the Krios, Mende, Loko, Limba, Kuranko, and Fula, just to name a few. Everyone had looked somewhat the same on my first day, all dressed in their school uniforms, but overhearing conversations in multiple languages confirmed that this was a mixed group. That put me at ease.

But I still had some worries and encountered some situations that made me feel like an outsider. My lack of language skills and desire to avoid trouble collided with each other as the first few days went by. I noticed that during class, everyone called our teacher "Mrs. Turner," but on the playground at recess they called her "Bob Lookers." Since I was struggling to grasp my first few Krio words, I wasn't sure which was her real name …but relatively quickly I realized that "Bob Lookers" was a nickname they'd given her because of her huge, thick glasses. I was glad to have figured that out before getting myself into a world of trouble.

During the second day at recess, I still tried to maintain a low profile by keeping to myself. I felt a little shy and apprehensive, still worried about making trouble or attracting attention. But I had my two housemates from Fatmata's house to help me, and their presence also helped me fit in faster. In fact, on that second day while I was standing with the two of them, a small group of other boys approached us and asked me to join their soccer game. I would have preferred to just watch from the sidelines, but they urged me to join with friendly insistence. Although I felt a little awkward doing so, I kicked the ball around with them until the bell rang. It was a little outside my comfort zone, but I was relieved to have been offered this gesture of welcome by my schoolmates.

Although English is the official language spoken at Sierra Leone's schools, Krio—which is a form of broken English—was spoken by nearly all the tribes. That was the first language I began to grasp, although I struggled with it somewhat. At home in Robomp Bana, everyone spoke Temene so I'd never needed to learn another language. But here in Freetown, all the tribes of Sierra Leone lived together. Since each tribe had its own language, Krio developed as a sort of bridging language. This broken-English hybrid was created so that anyone from any tribal background can easily pronounce its words, so it was favored in this melting pot of a city.

I had difficulty learning Krio at first, not because it was complex but because I was too shy to speak and didn't have a way to practice what I was learning. But the group of boys who talked to me on my second day helped me, in time, to overcome my shyness. They encouraged me to talk, asked me questions, and never made fun of me when I misspoke. As the days, weeks, and months passed I understood more of the Krio language. And the more I spoke Krio, the closer I got to speaking English.

Primary school students in Sierra Leone are required to learn all of the basic subjects, but once they move on to secondary school they're given more flexibility. I enjoyed learning tremendously and gobbled up information about every subject. The longer and harder I studied, the more I enjoyed my time at school.

After just a few months, I could feel my self-confidence growing. I was no longer the scared, apprehensive little boy who had walked clumsily through the front door on that first day of school. With time and experience, I began to realize that I was smart and capable. I didn't have to mimic what everyone around me was doing because I understood the teacher's instructions. I didn't have to avoid contact because I knew how to communicate with my fellow students. I didn't have to read the teacher's lips when she spoke because I was making strides toward being able to read, write and speak English fluently. I felt myself growing into a new person, one who was smarter and braver than I had ever hoped I could become.

My mother would come to Freetown about once per month to check on me, and I was always glad to see her. As much as I was growing and learning, it was a relief to have a little bit of home come right to me. I did my best to tell her how happy and grateful I was.

"Mom, thank you for letting me stay here with Fatmata and go to school. I am learning so much, and I love it," I would say.

"I am so glad, Ansu," she responded, drawing me near. "Your father and I knew you needed a little more than we could give you back home. And it makes our hearts happy to see you thriving and growing and becoming the wise little man we always knew you could be."

Chapter 7

Lessons in Academia and in Life

Having spent the first 10 years of my life in a house full of siblings and activity, I was used to a bustling household environment. But living at my sister's home in Freetown was different. Cohabitating with the other boys felt natural and normal, like they were my adopted siblings. But Fatmata's home played host to more than just a gaggle of studious children.

My sister's husband was called Sorie Ibrahim Mansaray, but most people knew him by his nickname, "Shek Kabir." He was well recognized in the Islamic community in Freetown and also a successful and popular businessman. He owned two stores where he sold bags of rice, potatoes, peanuts, onions, and other goods. One of his stores was in Freetown about a 10-minute walk from where we all lived together, and the other was in the diamond mining area in Koidu Town.

Since he was so active in the community and so well-liked by his peers, his house had slowly become a center for business meetings and Islamic affairs. Business traders frequently came to the house from various parts of the country, eager to connect with Shek Kabir and seek his advice. They usually came at night to talk about business deals, and their lively conversations would stretch on toward the dawn.

As for Islamic affairs, Shek Kabir was one of the group leaders of the Temene mosque in Freetown. During Rabi-ul-Awwal, the annual celebration of the birthday of the Holy Prophet Mohammad, some of the celebrants would come to the house for meetings. He was a no-nonsense, get-things-done member of the congregation, organizing the parades and other activities for the occasion.

Whenever guests were in the house at night—whether temporarily to chat about business or overnight as part of a religious celebration—the other youngsters and I had to sit in the corners of the room and wait for everyone to leave. When the final stragglers had gone home, we would clear the living room and spread our mats on the floor to sleep. There was no telling how long the meetings would last, but we had no choice but to stay in the corners until they were over, where we would study quietly without getting in anyone's way. When guests decided to come calling on school nights, we all knew we'd be bone tired the next day and dozing in class.

At the beginning of my second year of schooling, I transferred to a public school called East End Municipal. I had loved my time at Hope Day School, but it was privately owned and very expensive to attend. East End Municipal's fees were lower, so switching made it financially possible to continue my education.

The school was two miles from Fatmata's house, but I enjoyed the daily walk and often met up with friends to make the journey there. And I found that acclimating to public school felt much less stressful than getting used to private school. Everything at East End Municipal was more relaxed, from classroom rules to teachers' expectations for their students. The academics were still rigorous, but nothing felt as stiff and confining as it had at Hope Day.

My very favorite thing about my new school? It had its own library where students could go after class to study and complete their homework. Doing homework at home was fine, but working on it surrounded by books felt so much more scholarly. Plus it was nice to have some time to myself, apart from the group of boys back home.

At East End Municipal I made tremendous progress and demonstrated scholastic excellence. One year, after the final exam results in standard two were announced, I was promoted to standard four, which was the equivalent of 7th grade level, and skipped standard three.

Before that double promotion, I was in standard one class, when my teacher took me to a standard two classroom to teach that class basic mathematics; addition, subtraction, multiplication and division. It was very unpleasant for me as I thought it would be offensive and humiliating for that class to be taught by someone who was one class below. My teacher decided I should teach the class that day to motivate the students to put more effort in their learning. According to my teacher, if a student from a lower class could teach a higher class, that should give them the clue they needed to move forward.

My books were my best friends, and I studied hard both at school and at home. At first, I did not socialize much with the other students. There were a few who wanted to be my friends, and it was difficult to avoid them when it became clear we had things in common. But I was very anxious to learn and succeed so that my parents, brothers, sisters and friends back in the village would be proud of me. Plus I had started school very late, and wanted to catch up with others of my age.

But after a while, I wanted more than my books could provide. I remained dedicated to my studies, but missed being social and started to make friends with those who had the same ambitions as me. The first of these friends was Abdulai Sesay, who came to Freetown from Bamoi Village to attend school. Abdulai and I were truly "birds of a feather," sharing a common goal, a common purpose and above all, we shared a common vision for the future. He soon became my best friend. I also met and befriended Ibrahim Wurie, who would be one of my closest friends for many years to come…and play an important role in my future path.

When I was attending school back in the 1960s, there was severe overcrowding in some of the primary schools in Freetown. Because of this, most schools sent their final year students to Model Municipal Primary School, a public overflow school. Model Municipal was a one-year school that focused solely on preparing students for the "selective entrance examinations," a series of tests that determined if a student would be promoted to secondary school or high school.

In 1965, I was among a group of students sent to Model School to prepare for the selective entrance examinations. Because it was only a one-year school that concentrated on exams, all teaching was accelerated.

There was no time to waste. Every student had to participate in the school work, do daily homework, study for regular tests and unannounced tests or face the possibility of failure and being retained. We all knew that classwork would be accelerated and that the stakes were high, so the relaxing atmosphere of East End Municipal was nowhere to be found here. It was intense, and the massive amounts of studying meant there wasn't much time left for fun. In fact, I and my classmates were always aware that we could be suspended at any time for below-average academic performance. We kept our heads down and focused on learning as much as we could as fast as we could.

Prior to the year-end exams, each student was required to choose three secondary or high schools and rank them in order

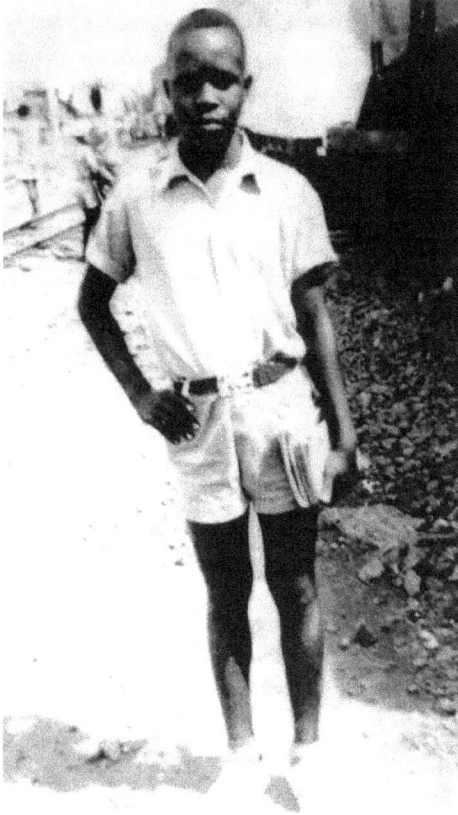

Attending Model Municipal Primary School Freetown,
Sierra Leone

of preference. This setup was created so each student had
the best chance of being accepted into a school of his
choice. If a student successfully passed the entrance
examinations but his first choice school was already full, the
second and third choices were all lined up. (Students who
failed would not move on. They had to repeat the one-year
program and retake the exams.)

I studied harder than I'd ever studied before for those selective entrance exams. And I passed.

I was placed in my first-choice school, Albert Margai High School, but after two years there I decided to transfer to Methodist Boys High School (MBHS). I wanted to be challenged and get the most out of my education, and the format at MBHS appealed to me for this reason.

The aim of MBHS was to develop students' abilities and talents by raising the standard of expectation. The subjects were similar to the ones I'd studied at Albert Margai, but MBHS required higher grades to be promoted from one level to another. Hard work, studiousness, and focus were expected from every student, as indicated by the school's Latin motto, *Laboramus expectantes*, "We labor and we expect."

I knew that picking a Methodist school would mean participating in Christian prayers every morning and foregoing my own Islamic traditions while on school grounds. In Sierra Leone, there are no special cases when it comes to faith in schools. Every school begins the day with some form of prayer, and every student participates. If you are a Muslim and opt to attend a Christian school, you will attend and participate in the morning assembly prayers. Likewise, if you are a Christian and choose to attend one of the few Arabic schools, you would be expected to take part in Islamic prayers throughout the day. I knew my faith was strong, so even though studying at MBHS meant conforming to Christian traditions, I wasn't upset or worried. My priority was getting the best education I possibly could, and I knew MBHS would help me achieve that goal.

Since the school was located outside the city of Freetown, a special passenger train was provided at no cost to the students. The train route started from downtown Freetown and made periodic stops through several stations to Kissy Mess Mess, the final stop. Pickup time at my station was 7 a.m.

Missing the train meant arriving late for class, and tardiness had serious consequences. Students who were present at the assembly hall for morning prayers were considered to be on time. Any student who arrived after morning prayer was considered late and subject to corporal punishment. The late students were met at the school entrance by a group of teachers who whipped them with canes.

In fact, the school system in Sierra Leone embraced corporal punishment for multiple purposes. At MBHS and elsewhere, teachers were empowered to cane students who violated school rules and regulations, or who performed poorly in the classroom.

Since I was desperate to succeed, lateness was not an option for me. I was one of the first to arrive at the train station every morning, often an hour before the train even arrived! And because of my good behavior and class performance, I was never subject to corporal punishment.

In fact, my good behavior and excellent grades earned me a spot as a prefect. This meant I was part of an elite group of senior students selected to assist the teachers in maintaining order in the classrooms. My prefect duties also included serving as a substitute teacher as needed. I loved teaching as much as learning, so I enjoyed this opportunity to flex my teaching muscles.

Classroom life was orderly and peaceful, but after-school sports were another matter.

Nearly all of the students in Freetown schools participated in some kind of sport, and we all took our games very seriously. Rivalries were common and fierce, and sporting matches could get wild and raucous.

Conduct on the field wasn't monitored very closely, so students on rival teams felt free to taunt and challenge each other before and during the games, in and out of the stadium. And when competition was over and a winner declared, fights broke out. The losing team typically got the fight rolling with the first few insults and punches, with the winning team joining in enthusiastically. Although the fights began in and around the stadium, they often spilled out into the streets of Freetown. If the situation became especially wild and violent, the police would step in to restore order.

I was not interested in fighting but had to learn to protect myself nonetheless.

MBHS students who attended sporting events to support our teams were required to wear our school uniforms. Inside the stadium we were seated by schools, and each school assigned teachers and prefects to monitor their students. But when the game concluded and tensions were high, the monitors had virtually no control over the students. Students associated with both winning and losing teams were easily visually identified by their uniforms, and anyone could be targeted.

Because of this dynamic, I never walked home alone after a sports event. Before attending inter-school events, I contacted classmates who lived in my home neighborhood to discuss and plan our return route. We settled on a meeting place to gather at the end of the game, and walked home together in a group. Lone students were easy targets, and we found strength and protection in numbers.

I had a tendency toward worry so these nerve-wracking walks home caused me quite a bit of stress. But those aside, I enjoyed the culture and structure I found at MBHS. The high learning standards suited me, and it felt good to be visibly successful at a prestigious school.

And I knew I was lucky to attend MBHS. Many boys my age were unable to attend school at all.

Pursuing education in Sierra Leone meant paying tuition. When I attended high school in the sixties, schools were very strict about collecting their fees. Students were expected to pay the fees on the first day of school, and those who did not pay were dismissed until the fees were collected.

Fee collection was a very public and sometimes humiliating process. At Methodist Boys High School, collection teams went from classroom to classroom with the delinquent list. As soon as the team entered a classroom, the teacher halted the lessons to allow the collection process. A team member called out the names of those who hadn't paid their school fees and asked them to leave the classroom and not return until the fees were paid. Those whose families could pay the fee returned at some point. Those who could not pay dropped out of school—either temporarily until the family could get the money together, or permanently if they could not.

School fees—both then and now—contribute to the high dropout rate in Sierra Leone. Students who begin school but are unable to complete their education are thrown into limbo. Jobs are always scarce and most dropouts are unable to find traditional work. Many of them turn to the notorious occupation of trading: They sell goods in local markets and elsewhere in the country.

Due to the collaborative efforts of my parents, Fatmata and her husband, and myself, I was fortunate to go through schooling in Freetown without any difficulty paying my school fees. At the end of harvest season my parents set aside several bags of rice to be sold for my tuition money. During the rainy season when crops were being planted and money was scarce, Fatmata and her husband took care of my school needs.

When my mother came to Freetown for her monthly visits, she always gave me a bit of money for school lunches. But instead of spending it on food, I saved it, month after month. When school closed for the long recess from late June through late September, I took all the lunch money I had saved and started a business.

I purchased bread, sugar, canned milk, and cookies and took them back to Robomp Bana to sell. These items were not available in the village, so they were exotic and exciting to my neighbors. After I sold all my pre-packaged goods, I used my profits to purchase bananas, eggs, coconuts, palm oil, and other items to bring back to the city. In Freetown, I wholesaled these items to local market traders who in turn sold them piece-by-piece to the general public.

By the time school started again, I had usually tripled my money. Without any reservations I gave it all to my guardians to be used for my school needs. My thriving business took all of my attention during school break every year until 1969. That year changed everything.

As my trading business became increasingly popular in Robomp Bana, I decided to expand to neighboring villages and enlist the help of my brother, Abdul Karim. During my school break in 1969, we loaded a boat with goods from Freetown and headed to Ro Gbonko, a village that is only accessible by sea. We left early that morning, paddling our heavy boat across the wide river.

The sky was partly cloudy that morning but there was no sign of rain and the river was calm. We paddled leisurely, chatting and gossiping and enjoying each other's company. After 40 minutes of paddling, we arrived safely at Ro Gbonko, tied the boat to a tree at the wharf, and started selling our goods door-to-door. By late afternoon, everything had been sold and we started buying bananas, eggs, palm oil, and coconuts to take back with us to Robomp Bana. The following day, we'd take these goods to Freetown and begin the process again. We loaded our boat and prepared to head home.

As we started the boat journey back to our village, the weather shifted ominously. Suddenly, the sky was covered with thick, dark clouds that blocked out the sun. My stomach knotted in worry as the calm river became choppy, then rough and turbulent with the high tide. Strong winds picked up out of nowhere, and seemed to be blowing in every direction all at once. As we fought to continue paddling, the wind created bigger and bigger waves. We were lifted up and down, carried skyward then crashing down into the water. The storm was so loud we couldn't hear each other, but Abdul Karim looked at me with wide eyes full of fear. But he gripped his paddle and bore down, never giving up.

We were within sight of the wharf when a huge wave hit our boat and flipped it. It plunged, nose-down, into the wild river.

Our purchases from the day were heavy, and began pulling the boat downward unstoppably. The thrust of the submerging boat was also pulling the two of us down into the deep river. I popped my head above water as soon as I got clear of the boat, but couldn't see my brother.

"Abdul Karim!" I called. "Where are you?"

Just as panic was about to overtake me, his small head bobbed above the surface a few feet away. My heart flooded with relief. He waved to me, and I motioned for both of us to head toward shore. The boat and our purchases were lost. We needed to save ourselves.

The swimming skills I'd learned in my early years paid off; Abdul Karim and I swam hard and fast through the rough waves until we made it to shore.

Ordinarily, the wharf would have been crowded with villagers waiting to buy fish from the fishermen, but it was deserted that day. The violent storm kept everyone away. If we hadn't been strong swimmers, we would have been lost; there was no one there to help us make it back to shore.

Although this was all bad luck and foul weather, it shook me to the bone. I had nearly died, and put my beloved brother's life at risk, too. My business as a trader had been prosperous and growing, but I couldn't face it any longer. My remaining school breaks were less profitable, but also less life-threatening!

Chapter 8

Dreams and Disasters

Many young people view education as a burden or a chore. I think this is more common among students growing up in cultures where schooling is an expected part of childhood. It's easier to take an education for granted if everyone around you is getting one, too. But even when I was growing up in Sierra Leone, during a time when education was both expensive and hard to come by, I encountered fellow students who slogged through each day with long faces, counting the minutes until classes let out and they could sprint to the soccer field to play.

But I saw my education as a blessing, from start to finish.

I certainly had days, even months, when school felt trying and overwhelming. As a gifted student, I was challenged by my teachers and pushed to excel at exams, so my stress level was pretty high. But I loved school, I was grateful to be there, and I soaked up knowledge like a plant thirsty for rain.

So when my years as a student began drawing to a close, I was sad. And a bit apprehensive. I had learned so much but knew I had much more to understand. And I was unsure what my next life steps would be.

During my final year of secondary school in 1971, I began to prepare for my general certificate of education exams. These extensive examinations are administered by the various secondary schools of Sierra Leone, but the exam papers are corrected by members of the national board of education. The board also decides if each student has passed or failed. Knowing that our own teachers would not be grading these exams made them even more daunting.

That final year felt different than all my previous years of schooling. Knowing that the graduation exams were on the horizon and that this might be my final year to prove myself as an exemplary student, I focused all my energy on studying. I abandoned all sports and other activities in favor of intense reading, writing, and memorization. Not since my days at Model School had I labored so hard. I considered nighttime—when everyone else was sleeping—to be the best time to study. I found it hard to concentrate during the daytime in the noisy, raucous environment of Fatmata's house. Tenants came and went all day, making a racket as they did, and although the other boys in the house had schoolwork, too, few were as serious as I. I even spent most of my weekends at quiet parks or at the MBHS library with my nose buried in my books.

A few friends would tease me about being so serious, but I ignored them. I believed education was the golden key that would open the door to a more dignified life. I had seen the difference education had made for many of the city-dwellers I'd met, and seen how many more opportunities they had than my friends, neighbors, and even family members back in the primitive farming village of my early childhood. I admired all of the educated people I met and studied them surreptitiously. Sometimes I walked the streets of Freetown alone, just observing people and their interactions. I watched well-to-do people shopping and chatting with each other. I noted how happy the adults who could afford to go to the cinema seemed to be. I noticed that office workers—especially government employees— appeared well-dressed and content as they walked to their jobs or drove their cars to work.

(As a side note, my admiration for people that owned cars back in Sierra Leone was beyond imagination. In my mind, anyone who owned a car had succeeded in life and possessed a strong financial foundation. I hoped fervently that someday I would own and drive my own car. And I clung to that hope like a lifeline.)

The older I grew and the more I learned, the clearer it became that I was driven to succeed myself. I wanted to be someone who was admired for his success, to the fullest extent of the word. I admired the educated, ambitious people I observed around me, and wanted to keep pace with them, wanted them to admire me in turn. I firmly believed that knowledge and book-learned wisdom would enable me to live a modern, civilized, successful life. So I threw myself, heart and soul, into my studies.

And it paid off. I successfully passed the general certificate of education examination and earned my high school diploma.

The day of my high school graduation was a joyful day in our house in Freetown. Unfortunately, Fatmata's husband, Shek Kabir, couldn't join in the celebrations because he was out of town on business but my sister, cousins, and I had a raucous meal together after my graduation ceremony. When Shek Kabir returned from his trip two days later, he announced that he, Fatmata, and I were all going to Robomp Bana together to celebrate my accomplishment with my family and neighbors! We packed quickly and departed the very next day.

It was overwhelming and heartwarming to be reunited with my whole family once more. My siblings eagerly greeted me with hugs and jokes, and there was much laughter and playful roughhousing. I could hardly believe how much they'd all grown! Brothers and sisters who'd been little children when I'd left were tall, chatty young adults now.

When I'd first left my home village for Freetown, it had been a somber, solemn time but my return to Robomp Bana after graduation was the exact opposite: I had never seen my family members so elated and carefree. My eldest brother, Abu, was especially happy since sending me to school had been his brainchild to begin with.

"I'm so proud of you, Ansu," he told me, throwing a heavy arm around my shoulders. "You've made us *all* proud."

My sisters and mother worked for an entire day preparing an enormous feast, with all the best foods our farm and village could provide. In the hours leading up to this celebratory meal, I'd been talking and laughing and rejoicing with my brothers and chatting with village neighbors about my experiences and life in the big city. I felt so welcomed and valued, it warmed my heart.

But a shadow of sadness was cast across this joyous affair. My father had passed away while I was attending school, many years before, and we all mourned his absence at this celebration. My mother shed many sorrowful tears, thinking about him that night. I can only imagine what my graduation from secondary school would have meant to him, had he lived to see it. He was not there in flesh and blood, but we knew his spirit had joined us as we ate and talked. We all missed him tremendously but did our best to live righteous lives every day, just as he would have wanted us to do.

Graduation from secondary school was a major step up for me, but I also knew it was merely the first of many steps I needed to take. That diploma may have started me on the path to success, but my journey was just beginning. And as I entered this new phase in my young adult life, I hoped with my whole heart that my journey would end at a specific destination: the United States of America.

Pursuing further studies in Sierra Leone was out of the question. Despite my stellar grades, I had very little chance of securing a scholarship or sponsorship to study at any of the universities in my home country. And my family certainly couldn't afford to pay the fees out of pocket. Finding work would be challenging, too. In the 60s and early 70s in Sierra Leone, nepotism, favoritism, and bribery ruled the economy. I knew no one who held a government position, I was not related to any government officials, and I had no money to bribe anyone in a position of power. This severely limited my employment options. As I considered these harsh facts, I came to the conclusion that seeking admission in an overseas university—privately and through my own personal efforts—was my best choice.

As I considered the various countries where I might apply to study, America immediately rose to the top of my list. It had always been considered the "promised land" by most residents of Sierra Leone, a place that overflowed with opportunity for anyone brave enough to make the journey. I had latched onto the idea of the American dream during my school days, and by graduation I felt that moving to this foreign land across the ocean was my destiny.

Of course, this didn't mean that I would forsake my homeland forever. There would always be room in my heart for the land of my birth. But I saw clearly how difficult it was for Sierra Leoneans to change their situations, how poor people were kept poor and rich people kept rich by countless official and unofficial systems. Opportunities were scarce, and the ones that existed were reserved for people who already led lives of privilege. I was smart but still a poor boy from a small village. I knew that if I was going to make something meaningful of my life, I would have to do it elsewhere.

And my heart told me that my own personal "elsewhere" would be in the United States.

Some people who yearn for success are not specific in their hopes and dreams. Whichever way the winds blows them, they go. I wasn't sure what my career might be or how my personal success would unfold, but I knew for certain where I wanted to be to pursue that success. I saw myself traveling across the Atlantic Ocean to the land of opportunity, to the land of the free, to America.

Of course, I'd never been to America. I only knew a couple of people who had ever visited this country so far across the sea from my homeland, including my best friend Ibrahim. But I fantasized endlessly about a life there. I had no idea how the people or cities or landscape would look there, but my mind returned to America over and over again. My imagination reached out to it endlessly, transformed it into the country that should someday be my home.

But I was no fool. I knew that finding my way to America would be difficult and frightening and expensive and challenging. To make this dream come true would be no easy task. But I never lost hope. I was desperate, determined, and focused. My dream of living in America was sparked during my early secondary school days, and that dream became stronger and stronger as the years passed by.

Before I had graduated from high school, I discovered another dreamer: My first cousin, Saidu Kamara.

It was 1967, and Saidu and I were both living in Freetown. He wasn't staying with my sister, choosing to live instead with another relative about three miles away from Fatmata's home. When I confessed my dream of moving across the ocean to the United States, he lit up.

"Yes," he said, his eyes bright. "Yes, Ansu, you should go to America. And you should take me with you. I've had the same dream for as long as I can remember. Let's find a way there together, yes?"

From that moment, we were inseparable.

Saidu was focused on securing study-abroad scholarships for the both of us. He believed that politicians were the key, that they controlled government-funded scholarships and that getting in their good graces would help us get the funding we needed to study in America. With that in mind, he suggested we participate in the general election process in Sierra Leone.

"If we help them win, how could they say no to our scholarship requests?" he said.

The day after Saidu revealed this plan, we marched our ambitious selves over to the main office of the All People's Congress (APC) party. There, we signed up as volunteers to be polling agents. Since the APC was desperate for interested individuals who wanted to serve the party in that capacity, we were accepted immediately. At that time, any native Sierra Leonean who was willing to volunteer without pay could join the party without any vetting or waiting period. The APC party's rival—and the long-time ruling party in my country—was the Sierra Leone People's Party (SLPP), and they were also looking for volunteers. Since our goal was to ingratiate ourselves to any politician with scholarship-related power, we could have joined either party. Although we both knew that many of our fellow Temene citizens were members of the APC, that had little impact on our decision. Our choice was based solely on our desire to befriend politicians in high places who might help us further our educations.

At the time we signed on as volunteers, the general elections were only two weeks away so both parties were working hard to connect with voters and change minds. During our first few days, we participated in an all-out campaign in Freetown. In the final week before the elections, my cousin and I were sent to the town of

Kamakwie in the Northern Province to serve as polling agents on behalf of APC candidate Edward Kargbo, who was in a hotly contested race.

We piled into an APC-owned minivan, and left Freetown for Kamakwie. Upon arrival, we joined a large group of campaigners already in town and together we intensified the campaign during those few remaining days. We campaigned door-to-door and village-to-village until the final day before the election. Then all of us were dispersed to various areas to officiate.

The night before election-day, Saidu and I were put on a bus to the village of Kagbayray, about 40 miles from Kamakwie. The roads were muddy and riddled with potholes and ditches, so a journey that should have taken about an hour and a half took four hours. We departed Kamakwie at 8 p.m. didn't arrive until a little after midnight. Because it was so late, the entire town was already asleep, and we couldn't find a thing to eat or drink. We were guests of the village chief, who greeted us sleepily and showed us to his guest house, which sported a hanging sheet instead of a door.

At about 6 a.m. on election-day, the chief woke us up for breakfast. We ate boiled cassava and drank bitter, black coffee. After thanking him for his hospitality, we reported to the building where the election was to be held to oversee the proceedings.

The election team had eight members. There were two uniformed police officers and two constables guarding the voting area, plus four polling agents, two from each party. Saidu and I—along with the agents from the SLPP— checked the names on the registration log to ensure the voter was who he or she claimed to be. After we collectively agreed to the validity of a name, that person was allowed to move on to the second step which was receiving a ballot card to vote. It was a fairly long and tedious process, but we took our duties seriously.

Late that evening, my cousin and I were transported back to our original base at Kamakwie. From there, we continued on and arrived back at Freetown after traveling all night.

On March 22, the morning after the election, I listened to the Sierra Leone Broadcasting Service (SLBS) on the radio, eager to hear news of the results. A reporter informed me that the APC had been triumphant over the SLPP in the 1967 election, marking the first time that a ruling party had lost an election in sub-Saharan Africa.

I shouted for joy.

"We did it. We won!" I laughed, thumping my hand on the table. Relief washed over me. This meant Saidu and I had aligned ourselves with the right party and could begin campaigning for scholarship support.

Hearing the ruckus, my cousins began crowding into the kitchen to find out what was happening. Soon the room was full of happy chatter.

"Look, Ansu," Wusu said, drawing back the kitchen curtains. Outside in the streets of Freetown, we saw people spilling out of their homes to dance and celebrate this historic victory.

"Let's go. Let's get out there and join them," I said. And so we did.

The energy was electric. All of Freetown's citizens seemed to be flooding the streets to express their joy at the historic news. The crowd was boiling over with merriment and jubilation. My cousins and I were swept up toward Kissy Road, the main highway that runs through Freetown, where we ran into Saidu who had been on his way to meet us at Fatmata's.

"Saidu, we're going to America," I said, my voice choked with emotion. We embraced tightly, convinced our mutual dream was about to come true.

The celebration continued throughout the day, winding its way through the entire city. By about 5 p.m., my cousins and I found ourselves at the gates of the prime minister's palace in central Freetown, where the dancing and singing was nearly as lively as it had been early that morning. We began to hear some loud, sharp bangs nearby, but assumed they were part of the festivities, fireworks or drums.

Then we saw the trucks.

Huge trucks packed with fully armed soldiers were parting the crowds, making their way toward the palace. And they were firing. Within a few minutes, these looming trucks had surrounded the entire building and were raining bullets in the air to disperse the crowd.

Shouts of joy changed to screams of panic.

The chaos was unstoppable. Thousands of people were seized with fear all at once, and every single one of them was trying to flee from the prime minister's palace. I had no time to find any of my cousins, or ensure their safety. It was clear I needed to get myself out of there fast, or risk being trampled or shot.

It was a horrific scene. A day of peace and joy had turned to a frenzy of terror. The crowd became a stampeding mob, crushing anyone who was too slow or weak to get out of its way as the stronger ones ran for safety. I was lucky to be young and strong myself, but the experience of running and tripping over innocent citizens and being unable to help them was surreal and sickening. The screams still haunt me.

I finally made it back to Fatmata's house on the east side of town, after an hour of frantic running, only to find myself locked out. Someone who'd either arrived home before me or stayed away from the crowd altogether had locked the front gate. Clearly, the fear of marauding soldiers and panicked citizens invading our space had prompted this decision. I scrambled up over the fence and rushed into the house, relieved to be safe at last.

But safety was an illusion now.

We soon learned that the APC had never had the chance to come to power in full. What we'd witnessed at the palace was army officers taking over the government. Several powerful members of the SLPP-run military were so threatened by the success of the APC that they believed our country was safer under military rule. And they were able to prevent the new government from becoming established. They quickly dissolved the legislature and suspended the constitution in a swift coup.

In the days and weeks that followed, Freetown was locked down. We were under strict curfew, forbidden to be out of doors before 6 a.m. or after 6 p.m. Soldiers patrolled every inch of the city, day and night, just looking for someone to step out of line. They broke up soccer games, dispersed groups of people socializing in the street, did everything they could to make us feel powerless and afraid.

It was hard to get news of what was really going on within the government, but the SLBS broadcast whatever they could and we got some details through word of mouth. A neighbor told us that newly elected APC Prime Minister Siaka Stevens had been placed under house arrest just minutes after taking his oath of office. Then we got word that Stevens and a few other APC party members had escaped to neighboring Guinea. It was hard to tell truth from rumor, but I held out hope that Stevens was planning his return to power from afar.

The upheaval was astonishing, and the lives of Freetown's citizens were upended. Saidu and I recognized that these changes were appalling and disturbing for our countrymen, but also secretly mourned our own situations. The coup put our plans to campaign for American scholarships on hold. Indefinitely.

The 1967 military coup was a shock to many dreamers, including my cousin and me. Our peaceful, happy lives in Freetown were turned upside down. Armed men were suddenly everywhere, and the strict curfews limited our ability to move freely. Within a few weeks, we began to struggle with food shortages since traders who would ordinarily bring their goods into the city to sell were now too afraid to even approach Freetown's borders. In fact, getting in or out of the city was nearly impossible. The military had set up numerous checkpoints along the main roads into and out of Freetown, and most residents didn't even attempt to pass through them all. We were prisoners in our own homes, constantly monitored and scrutinized by the gun-carrying soldiers that surrounded us. I was always afraid. And being on high alert all day every day was exhausting.

Fortunately, the military government was destined for a short run.

An opposing group of high-ranking military officials wanted to return Sierra Leone to civilian rule, recognizing that a makeshift martial government was unsupportable. Most citizens weren't aware of this until much later, but this group was carefully and strategically planning another coup to overthrow recently installed military leader Andrew Juxon-Smith and his cronies. They were acutely aware that the penalty for a failed coup was death by hanging, and had seen that kind of harsh justice carried out time and again after unsuccessful attempts to overthrow the seated leader. They were cautious and meticulous, aware that winning was not optional.

On April 18, 1968—a year and a month after the military coup—this group enacted its own coup. Calling themselves the Anti-Corruption Revolutionary Movement and led by John Amadu Bangura, they stormed the governmental strongholds. Military leaders were imprisoned, and other army and police officers were stripped of their power.

Once the constitution was restored, Siaka Stevens, the APC party leader, was recalled to Sierra Leone to take his seat as prime minister. He formed and headed a new civilian government and our candidate, Edward Kargbo, became cabinet minister. Celebrations broke out across the nation, but those of us in the capital city celebrated the most enthusiastically. We hoped this change in leadership would mean a return to normal life in Freetown, and thankfully, it did.

Shortly after the civilian government came to power, Saidu became mysteriously ill. He lost weight rapidly, deteriorated quickly, and none of the doctors were able to settle on a diagnosis. It was terrifying and heartbreaking to see him in decline. No one knew what to do. One day he looked bad, but the following day he looked even worse. Words cannot fully express the misery I felt at seeing my dear cousin so gravely ill.

To the great sorrow of the family, friends, and neighbors who knew this kind-hearted, gentle, humble young man, Saidu died after just a short period of illness. He was only 20 years old.

After his death, my interest in government scholarships was irrevocably tarnished. I simply could not imagine going that route without my cousin, the bright heart who had initially suggested we pursue scholarships as a means of getting ourselves overseas. I never followed up with our candidate, Edward Kargbo, to see if he could help me study abroad, nor did I discuss our scholarship plans with any government official. I would have to find another way.

And although I was discouraged, disturbed, and disappointed, I never gave up hope for the future. I was determined to pursue other avenues, to find a way to achieve our dream of living in the United States. I thought of Saidu often and firmly believed that if he could speak to me from heaven, he would have told me to continue the struggle and never give up.

He was greatly missed. His sudden departure from the face of this earth left sorrowful memories of him etched upon my heart forever. But his memory drove me onward, toward the realization of our shared dream.

I had limited resources and was one of thousands of Sierra Leoneans who wanted to immigrate to America. I knew a few school friends who'd moved to the U.S. in the early 70s, but had no specific vocation or skills to bring to a new nation. The odds were stacked against me. But I never allowed any obstacles to divert my attention or negative thoughts to dampen my dream.

Henry Ford once said, "Whether you think you can or you can't, you're right." I lived by that motto and focused all my efforts on hope and optimism. I wanted the best for my life, and I searched high and low for the path that would lead me in that direction.

Hope was my fuel, my guiding light, my beacon. In the dark aftermath of my beloved cousin's death, hope was the star that showed me the way.

Chapter 9

Waiting in Limbo

Although I clung to hope like a life raft, I couldn't help but feel a bit stuck. I was still living with my sister in Freetown, but her house was no longer filled with the raucous sounds of eight energetic schoolboys. There were only three of us left, including myself. The others had all graduated from secondary school, given humble thanks to Fatmata and Shek Kabir, and left the house to seek their own fortunes. I lingered behind, quietly plotting my future life in America.

While I was waiting and planning and scheming, I occupied my time by earning as much money as I possibly could. I wasn't sure how I would get myself across the ocean, but I'd need some cash to make the trip possible. I was a hard worker and a smart young man, but refused to settle on a full-time or long-term job since I didn't want to put down roots in Sierra Leone. Instead, I took a series of smaller, part-time jobs and cobbled together a decent living for myself in Freetown.

Several of my jobs were travel or transportation-oriented. I washed taxicabs for 50 cents per taxi. At Jnet Wharf, I assisted passengers with their luggage and was paid one leone per day by the boat owners (the equivalent of about 75 U.S. cents). I worked as a conductor for a Poda Poda driver from Freetown to Wellington on the outskirts of the city. Poda Poda is one form of local transportation which consists mainly of refurbished mini-vans that transport people around Freetown. They operated more or less like public buses, with set routes and regular stops. The vans were often overloaded because they were the cheapest means of traveling from one area to the other. It only cost 25 cents per trip in the 1960s. As a conductor, my job was to collect the money from the passengers when they reached their destination. At the end of each day the Poda Poda drivers usually paid me five leones (about $3.75 U.S.).

Not wanting to let my education go to waste, I also took on night tutoring work. I started by assisting two primary school boys with their homework on a nightly basis, but as word spread throughout my neighborhood I found myself adding more and more students. Within a short period, my class of two students quickly increased to 15. At the end of the week, I collected one leone per student from the various parents who eagerly funded my tutoring business.

In my extremely limited free time, I honed my skills on the soccer field. Soccer is considered not only a sport but a way of life in Sierra Leone, and I'd played well and excelled during my school days. As a young adult, I boosted my abilities by playing hard and intensely whenever I had the chance.

At this point in my life, I could have built a career for myself in Freetown in any number of ways. I had gained business acumen during my stint as a trader between school years, and could have secured a lucrative office job. I was a skilled tutor and could have become a valued school teacher. My talent for soccer could have secured me a position on a professional team. But none of these options appealed to me. My physical body may have been in Sierra Leone, working day and night to accumulate much-needed cash, but my mind and thoughts were across the vast, blue Atlantic Ocean. I dreamed of my Promised Land every free moment of every day.

To me, everything I was capable of doing in Sierra Leone was irrelevant. If I had wanted to stay in my home country, there was no doubt in my mind that I would have put my heart and soul into whatever I chose to do. But I didn't want to stay. All I wanted was to achieve my dream of going to America. I firmly believed that was the only thing that could lead to my true happiness and deep personal satisfaction. Every fiber of my being yearned to begin my journey to my future home.

Sometimes in the late afternoon I walked up to Flat Stone, an area atop some low hills on the eastern side of Freetown. Residents often went there to fly kites, or to watch the sun set over the horizon. I cast my eyes westward, in the direction of the United States, and let my hopes unfurl out from my chest and through the evening air toward the place I longed to be.

To learn more about the Promised Land, I made frequent visits to the American embassy in Freetown. There, I read bulletins, books, brochures, anything I could get my hands on that contained precious information about the United States. New York, Texas, and California were the top three states I was interested in. I learned that those three states were the largest in terms of size and population, and I wanted to live somewhere with lots of space, lots of people, and lots of opportunity. I also focused on those three states because a few of my secondary school classmates had secured university admissions there, so I figured if I could relocate to New York, Texas, or California, I could reunite with my friends. I plied the embassy workers with questions until they shooed me away, and tucked myself into corners to read and research until the building closed for the night. My hunger for anything American was voracious.

On Saturday afternoons, if I was not too busy, I would head over to the Odeon or Roxy Theater in Freetown to watch Western movies. It was the golden era of the Western, so many of the films I watched starred legends like John Wayne and Kirk Douglas. After watching a good cowboy movie, I felt as if I had just been to Texas. The stark beauty of the landscapes I glimpsed in those action-packed movies kept my hopes alive. I also scoured every news source I could—from the Sierra Leone Broadcasting Service and Sierra Leone Daily Mail newspaper, to the BBC and materials at the American embassy—hungry for news about American celebrities beloved in the sixties, including Elvis Presley, Cassius Clay (now Mohammed Ali), James Brown, and Redd Foxx.

If the preoccupations of the mind could be seen on the face, any passing stranger would have known what was going on inside me. But in reality, I kept my dreams to myself. I joked with friends, collaborated with pals and cousins on the occasional job, and played soccer with neighbors and friends. But none of them knew about my future plans, none of them saw the strong force pulling me west toward America. I chose this inner solitude, chose to keep my plans secret, even though I occasionally longed to shout them from the rooftops. Then I'd look around me, see how small and limited life in Freetown appeared, and bit my tongue.

Very rarely, I'd consider my options in Sierra Leone and feel a slight pull. My family was here, my friends were here, everything I'd ever known was here. I had the skills and intelligence and connections needed to create a thriving career. It would have been relatively easy to build a prosperous, comfortable life right where I was living.

But my heart would not have it. I didn't know if it was my true destiny to live in America, or just my own innate stubbornness. But it didn't matter. The drive was too strong, the pull irresistible. Whatever the reason, I knew I had to find a way.

And soon, I would.

Chapter 10
From Dream to Reality

As the days, weeks, and months continued to roll by and another dry season was coming to a close, I knew it was time to take action. I had been waiting and saving money and researching for long enough. I was becoming anxious with anticipation, and weary of living my life in a holding pattern.

Luckily, it was around this time that I got some extraordinary good news from my friend Ibrahim Wurie.

In the mid-1960s, Ibrahim and I had attended school together and lived in the same neighborhood in Freetown. He'd been one of the first friends I made at school, and remained one of my closest friends as we grew up together. We studied together and both had naturally ambitious dispositions, but our bond went beyond schoolwork. We played countless games of soccer together at the Freetown parks, and went to the professional soccer games together to cheer on our favorite teams. We visited each other frequently during those days. Ibrahim's parents liked me and everyone at my house welcomed him with open arms.

In 1970, Ibrahim immigrated to the United States to further his education. His family, the Wuries, was extremely powerful, wealthy, and well-known throughout Sierra Leone. They ran big businesses, owned fabulous homes, and held important positions in government. In fact, one of Ibrahim's uncles was a cabinet minister in Siaka Stevens' administration, and he helped my friend make is way to New York. Despite his privilege, Ibrahim was down-to-earth, earnest, and good-hearted. Before he left Sierra Leone, he promised me that if all went well for him in America, he would do everything in his power to make sure I was able to join him there.

In 1972, after two years in the U.S., Ibrahim kept his promise.

I remember so clearly the day that I received that thick yellow envelope from him, his messy handwriting on the front and the exotic looking postage stamps covering one side. I had no idea what he'd sent me, but somehow knew it was something significant, and tore open the envelope with shaking hands.

Inside, I found a note from Ibrahim. It read:

Dear Ansu,

Just as I promised, I've found a way to get you over to America. I have applied on your behalf to the RCA Institute of Technology, a private college in New York City that offers two year associate degrees and certificates for education in technology, business, engineering. And they've accepted you!

I've taken care of all the application fees myself, so all you have to do is complete the enclosed forms and mail them in. They include an I-20, which is required by the American embassy for you to obtain a student visa. You'll also need to find a sponsor, but I'm sure you'll have no trouble with that.

I look forward to studying and celebrating with you in New York soon!

Your friend,
Ibrahim

I held his letter, the forms, and the admission materials in my trembling hands and let my tears fall freely. Soon I was sobbing with joy and relief, and collapsed into a chair with my arms folded on the tabletop. Thanks to my generous friend's help, I could see a clear path to achieving my goal. Obstacles were falling away, and in the time it had taken to read Ibrahim's letter, I felt myself move closer to my destiny.

I could move to New York. A new life awaited me there.

But first I had to tell my family of my plans. All this time, I'd kept my dream of relocating to America a secret from Fatmata, her husband, my mother and brothers, everyone except Ibrahim and my now-departed cousin Saidu.

The night after I'd received Ibrahim's life-changing letter, I sweated my way through dinner and finally mustered the courage to make my announcement. I told them how I'd dreamed of moving to America for many years, about working with Saidu and the disappointment that followed, and how my endless string of jobs had all been to save money to relocate.

"Today, I heard from my friend Ibrahim Wurie," I said, my voice shaking a little. "He's been studying in New York, and he knows how much I want to join him in America. He has secured admission for me at a school called the RCA Institute of Technology and even paid my fees. So now I can go. I can move to America."

Looking at their wide-eyed faces, I had no idea what to expect. Would they be angry that I'd concealed this from them? Sad that I was leaving?

"Oh Ansu," Fatmata breathed, brushing a tear from her cheek. "What *wonderful* news!"

I let out a breath I didn't realize I'd been holding, and laughed. Soon we were all laughing, and Shek Kabir and the boys were congratulating me and thumping me on the back. Everyone was happy, and I was so relieved.

"We must celebrate!" Shek Kabir said.

"Well, yes…but we might want to wait a bit," I said. "The school has accepted me, but I still have to find a fiscal sponsor and get all the paperwork in order. This is really just the first step."

And it was. Even though Ibrahim had cleared the path, I still had to take it. And that meant completing those forms and ensuring everything was set from my end. So the following day, I began doing the necessary work to secure my student visa. Receipt of the admission materials from RCA Institute of Technology was just the first step. I still had much to do.

As Ibrahim had mentioned, I'd need to find a sponsor; a person, group, or organization that would assume financial responsibility for me while I studied in the United States. Since my father had passed away and my mother was a poor woman with many children to support, I could not expect financial assistance from my immediate family. My mother would have loved to give me anything I needed to make my dream come true, and I knew she was unspeakably proud of everything I'd accomplished already. But while she offered me endless love and support and prayers, she simply didn't have the resources to sponsor me.

Knowing this, I realized that finding a sponsor might be quite challenging. I might connect with the perfect person in just a few days and be on my way to the U.S. before the dry season had ended...or it might be weeks, months, or even years before I found the financial support I needed. Undeterred, I began reaching out to my more distant relatives, tactfully searching for someone willing to help me secure my visa.

Eventually, I started talking with my Uncle Massa Kamara, my father's brother.

Uncle Massa lived in Freetown and was considered fairly well-to-do. He was socially recognized and worked for many years as a ferry captain for the Sierra Leone Port Authority. Privately, he owned a few taxis that were making enormous amounts of money. He had seen that the public transit options in Freetown were inadequate to meet demand, and began his taxi service to fill that need. Other workers and government employees were paid once per month, but a busy taxi can make a month's salary in a single day. And his taxis often did just that.

One evening I decided to pay a visit to my uncle in Kline Town, a neighborhood in Freetown. I took my admission documents to the RCA Institute to show him that I had been admitted and was serious about furthering my education in the United States. My heart was hammering as I arrived at his door.

We chatted for a while, updating each other on our recent doings and laughing over a recent soccer match. Then I took a deep breath, and began my pitch.

"Uncle, I think you know how serious I've always been about my education," I began. He nodded for me to continue. "Well, I am trying to take it to the next level now. I've been accepted at a college in New York City and am working to secure my student visa."

"That's wonderful, Ansu! Congratulations," he said, beaming at me from his armchair.

"Thank you, I am very excited and pleased," I said, trying to keep my heart from pounding its way out of my chest. "But in order to get the visa, I need a sponsor. Someone has to support me financially while I study. Uncle, moving to America has been my dream for longer than I can remember, and you know my mother would sponsor me if she could...but she just doesn't have the resources. I'm hoping you'd consider being my sponsor."

His smile faded a little, and he widened his eyes at me.

"Well, you know, I would love to help you out, but I'm retired now from my job with the Port Authority. The only income I have is from the taxis," Uncle Massa told me, levelly.

"Yes, I know."

"And I've had to put much of my own earnings toward treatments for my diabetes. So between medical expenses and keeping my own family afloat, I don't have as much money to throw around as I used to!"

"I understand," I said, my heart sinking.

A long moment passed in silence while he looked me over.

"But…I appreciate the opportunity you've brought to me. You're a smart young man and I think you have great potential. If the taxi business continues to improve, I'd be delighted to sponsor you. But we'll have to wait and see."

"Thank you, Uncle," I said. "Thank you for considering this request."

He hadn't said "yes," but he also hadn't said "no." I left his home that night cautiously hopeful.

But then, disaster struck.

About two weeks later on a very rainy day, one of his taxis was chartered by two passengers to take them to the east ferry terminal. They were planning to board a ferry that would take them across the river to Lungi International Airport where they'd catch a flight for Europe.

The driver rushed through the busy and overcrowded streets in Freetown, which were flooded and slick from the rain. As he made a sharp turn, the driver lost control of his taxi and crashed into a guttered ditch. There were no fatalities, but the driver banged his head on the dashboard and was knocked unconscious both passengers suffered serious injuries.

My uncle's fiscal stability hinged on his taxi business, and this incident would cost him dearly. Disappointed, I decided to let go of my hopes that he would sponsor my student visa.

I briefly considered pursuing a scholarship. During the sixties and beyond, the Sierra Leonean government regulated and awarded scholarships to those who qualified, and some scholarships could be used for overseas study. But even though my grades were admirable, the requirements to obtain these scholarships were incredibly rigorous. I knew I was better off trying to find private sponsorship.

A few months passed, and more conversations with relatives proved fruitless. My dream of moving to America seemed to be fading away, since every path I pursued led me to a dead end.

Then a new, unexpected, and downright miraculous option presented itself in the form of my older brother Abu.

Since his recovery from smallpox, Abu had been working tirelessly to turn the family rice farming into a lucrative business. He employed several workers on the farm and, as a result, he harvested rice in abundance. Rice is Sierra Leone's main food, so the demand is always high. In the months leading up to my quest for a visa sponsor, Abu had become a major supplier for rice stores in Freetown and other towns. He quickly built up good financial capital, and was on his way to being a successful businessman.

Two days after I'd broken the news, my sister Fatmata headed back to Robomp Bana to inform the rest of our family herself. I'd already let her know that I was planning to approach Uncle Massa about sponsorship, but had no idea that she wanted to consult with Abu on the same subject. She knew more about his recent success than I did, and had a feeling he might be in a position to help me. By the time she'd returned, I'd already had my conversation with our uncle and knew my chances with him were slim. Fatmata didn't say a word about what had passed between her and Abu.

But about a week later, he showed up in Freetown.

I assumed he was there on business, since he came through the city more and more often to meet with his partners. Whenever he was in town, Abu would ask me to accompany him to the market so he could buy a few things to bring back home to the village. The day after he arrived, we were making the journey to the market, when he suddenly stopped walking.

"Let's go by the city park and have a talk," he said with a twinkle in his eye. "What do you say?"

"Sure," I replied, suspicious but totally ignorant of his motives.

The city park is located in central Freetown and has long been a gathering spot for city residents. People sit at the picnic tables and benches to talk and eat their lunches. Others meditate in the peaceful setting, or ride bikes through the park. As we headed toward it, I saw Abu smiling and wondered what on earth could be on his mind.

Before we arrived, Abu steered us into a little convenience store to pick up two bottles of 7Up and a few cookies to snack on. He paid quickly, and we continued on toward the park.

Within a few minutes, we were seated at a picnic table munching the cookies and swigging our sugary sodas. I kept sneaking glances at him, dying to ask what was going on, but held my tongue. I caught him looking directly at me, he held my gaze for a moment…and then he burst out laughing.

Well, I thought to myself, *whatever he's going to tell me is bound to be something good! Otherwise he wouldn't be cackling like that before he even breaks the news.*

"I heard about your American dream," Abu said, grinning. "Fatmata told me."

"Yes, I knew she would. That's why she went back to visit you and Mom."

"Well, I am so happy for you, Ansu. This is a dream worth following," he said. "Everyone will miss you, even more than when you left Robomp Bana for Freetown, myself included…"

"Abu, wait," I said, holding up a hand. "It is not a sure thing. I still have to find a sponsor, someone to help me cover my expenses. I've asked Uncle Massa, but he can't do it, so I'm still searching for someone."

"No, you're not. I've got it under control."

He explained how the rice business was booming, and that in his current financial position, he'd be able to sponsor me himself.

"That is, if you'll let me be your sponsor," he said through that big grin of his.

Speechless, I stood up and embraced him. For so many weeks, my dream of going to the United States had seemed like a fantasy, an illusion, a figment of my imagination. Now, suddenly, it was a reality. Excitement, relief, and pure joy flooded through me. As Abu thumped my back and told me how proud he was, I felt like I might pass out.

But the next day, I sprang into action. With Abu's support, I assembled all the required documents, including the sponsorship papers, and took them directly to the American embassy. An embassy worker reviewed them to ensure everything was complete, and then scheduled an applicant interview for me a few days later. During the interview, I met with an embassy employee who asked me about my reasons for traveling, and discussed some particulars about New York State and New York City to prepare me for my arrival. Then, within a week, I was issued an F-1 visa to go to the United States of America as a student.

On the first of May 1972, I departed from Sierra Leone and headed toward John F. Kennedy International Airport in New York City.

My new life was finally beginning.

Chapter 11

Arrival

When I've talked with friends about my journey to America, many of them told me how brave I was to leave home. I'm always honored by their praise but must say I felt more determined than brave. I'd never been on an airplane before, never left Sierra Leone before, never lived in anywhere outside of Africa before, and never taken such a long and momentous journey alone. As I boarded the jet, I did my best not to feel scared. I told myself that the roaring engines and stomach-clenching sensations I encountered on the plane were fascinating, not frightening. I tried to consider the idea of arriving as a stranger in a strange land as invigorating, not intimidating. Of course, it helped to know that Ibrahim would be there to help me get acquainted! Mostly I felt energized and hopeful, knowing my dream was finally coming true, but I was also extremely nervous. Determined to make my way in this new land of opportunity, grateful that I was finally fulfilling my destiny, and steeped in pure joy and eager anticipation…but also wrestling with unshakable fear and apprehension.

When the pilot announced that we needed to fasten our seatbelts in preparation for the 747 aircraft to touch down at

Kennedy Airport, I realized I was about to meet the "real" America. All I knew of my new home country had come from books and movies. How would actual New York be compared to the New York in my mind? I was about to find out.

After we landed at JFK Airport and disembarked, I was so nervous both my legs were shaking. I took deep breaths to calm my nerves, but everything felt so strange and foreign. The first thing I noticed was that the entire airport was enclosed. I couldn't see the sky or hear the earth-shaking noise that planes made as they were landing and taking off. A little disoriented, I made my way down a long tunnel to an immigration checkpoint, which was my first stop. After my documents were cleared, I continued to customs and the baggage claim area to grab my luggage. Everything moved slowly and it took several hours to get all the approvals I needed, but I was patient. Finally, I picked up my heavy suitcase and dragged it toward the nearest exit, ready to see the real America.

But I was stopped short.

The doors were opening automatically as people walked toward them. I had never seen or used this type of door before, and was more than a little baffled. I decided to stand to the side and watch the people walk through, hoping I'd be able to detect what was triggering them. The doors never closed on anyone, but I didn't want to become their first victim of the day. After several minutes of lurking, I had no clear answer and became impatient. I just decided to follow the lead of others and walk out with a group of people. *Thanks to God*, I thought as I walked through, and the doors slid open to let me out. It was painless, and I was relieved.

My next task was to get to Ibrahim Wurie's house in Queens. I had sent him a telegram to inform him of the date and time of my arrival, but he had not responded and was nowhere to be seen at JFK that day. I was hoping he would meet me at the airport, but assumed he was tied up elsewhere. (I found out later that the telegram arrived quite late, after I'd already arrived at his home in person!)

Alone and unsure, I figured I'd better make my own way to his house. As I stood on the grimy airport sidewalk watching cars whiz by me, a yellow cab pulled up. I peered inside, hoping to see my friend, but it was empty. A few days before departure, Abu and I had visited a Barclay's Bank in Freetown and exchanged Sierra Leone currency for American dollars, so I had the right type of money with me. I mustered my courage and rapped on the passenger window.

"Hello," I said nervously. "I need to get to Bedell Street in Queens, which is about five miles from here. How much would it cost to take me there?"

"This is a metered cab," the driver said gruffly. "The meter calculates the cost."

"Oh," I said. "I'm not familiar with metered cabs. Can we agree upon a fixed price instead?"

"You're new here, aren't you?" he asked, not unkindly.

"I am. Just arrived from Africa."

"OK, kid, get in. We'll say one dollar per mile."

I had no idea if this was a fair rate but felt like I had no other choice. So I climbed into the musty, dark interior of the cab and we set off for Queens.

The driver pulled onto an expressway almost immediately, and I was overwhelmed by the sheer number of cars whizzing past my window. Four crowded lanes on each side, both packed with cars driving in both directions. I couldn't see the famous New York City skyline from where we were, but I saw more buildings, vehicles, and billboards in those first few minutes than I'd seen in my whole life in Sierra Leone. After about three miles, the driver exited the freeway and headed into a residential area. Soon huge trees threw shade onto the streets, and the sidewalks were bordered by tall, narrow houses. I was astonished by how closely the taxi driver followed the street signs! He stopped at every stop sign, followed the traffic lights meticulously, and yielded when a sign instructed him to do so. Back in Freetown, signs like this were always treated as "suggestions" more than "laws," especially by cab drivers who always seemed to be in a rush to drop off one fare and collect another.

I was surprised to see almost no people; the area seemed deserted. No one was walking with their children, running errands, standing in front of their homes talking with neighbors. Back in Freetown, there was no getting away from people. They flooded the neighborhoods, streets, market places, parks, everywhere you looked you'd see people. You practically had to shove them out of your way to get down the street sometimes! Seeing these silent, vacant-seeming streets was almost eerie to me.

The very moment that the cab pulled up in front of his house, Ibrahim Wurie pulled in right behind us. He was just returning from school and was extremely surprised to see me.

"You're here!" he said excitedly, embracing me and thumping me on the back. "I had hoped to meet you at the airport."

"I'd hoped for that, too!" I said, laughing.

"Let me get your bag. Let's go inside."

Ibrahim was living in a single-family home with two bedrooms and a basement. I was curious to know how he'd secured this cozy little setup for himself.

"Ibrahim, how on earth did you end up in this house all by yourself?" I asked, as we hauled my bags through the front door.

"By being a good Samaritan!" he told me, flashing a smile.

It turns out that he'd been living in an apartment complex a ways down Bedell Street, which was fine but a bit crowded. One day he had been at a nearby grocery store, and noticed an elderly white lady struggling with her groceries. He rushed over and offered to help her.

"Can I give you a hand, ma'am?" Ibrahim asked, settling her bags into her rickety hand-cart. "Let me help you get these home."

He told her he had come to New York from Sierra Leone to study and was living up the street. It turned out she lived just a block from the store, and as they walked together—Ibrahim pushing her cart and carrying her extra items—he told her he'd be happy to help her out any time she needed someone to pick up groceries for her.

"You're such a kind young man," she'd said gratefully.

From that day on, she'd call him up whenever she had a list of items she needed. Ibrahim would stop by her house to collect the money, then bring back everything on her list, and even help her put everything away in her kitchen. After a few months, she grew to trust and rely on him. She was the mother of two grown children, one of whom lived on Long Island relatively nearby, and the other of whom had moved out of state. Ibrahim could tell she was lonely, missing her children, so he began helping her more and more, doing chores around the house and occasionally mowing the lawn. Eventually the grown children stopped home to visit their mother and met Ibrahim. The whole family grew to love and depend on him, to the point that when the children decided it was time for their mother to move into an assisted living facility, everyone agreed that Ibrahim should move into the house on Bedell Street.

"They asked me to pay a tiny amount of rent—half of what I'd been paying for the apartment—and I agreed!" he told me. "I couldn't be happier."

He showed me to the second bedroom in the house and let me get settled while he started cooking our dinner. That night we ate, listened to African music, and talked for hours. We reminisced about our school days together and memories from long ago. It was midnight before I dropped into bed, exhausted.

My first full day in America began the day after I arrived. Ibrahim Wurie headed out for school and work, and I was left to my own devices. A little afraid to leave the house, I sat near the upstairs bedroom window and watched Bebel Street as far as my eyes could see. I wanted to go out exploring, but I was terrified that I wouldn't be able to find my way back. As I peered out the window what struck me most was the quiet. I had imagined all of New York to be noisy and bustling—similar to virtually every residential area in Sierra Leone—but Queens was actually quite peaceful. A few cars rolled past, and I saw some people walking their dogs, but during the day Ibrahim's street was mostly empty and incredibly quiet.

I arrived on Wednesday and continued observing Queens in solitary silence until Saturday when Ibrahim Wurie had time off to take me sightseeing. That morning we ate breakfast at the house in Queens, then headed to the subway station. Ibrahim wanted me to become familiar with the trains since I would be taking them to commute to school. As we stood on the platform, we peered at a map and he gave me a quick lesson on the lettered and numbered train lines before we hopped on an E train bound for Manhattan.

"New York is divided up into five enormous neighborhoods called boroughs," he told me as we waited. "We are in Queens, but there's also Manhattan, Brooklyn, the Bronx, and Staten Island. Today, we'll try to visit all five boroughs so you can get an overview of the entire city."

"And this train connects them all?" I asked.

"It does. The subway system is enormous and can take you almost anywhere in New York. Ah, here comes our train!"

A sleek, silver car was streaking toward us, its brakes screeching as it slowed to a stop. The doors slid open, and we walked on.

Although I had taken trains back in Sierra Leone, none of them had been this modern or fast! The experience was a little dizzying. The train rocketed through the neighborhoods of queens, headed west toward Manhattan. Buildings, trees, streets, and cars blurred by in my vision, and the huge, open sky floated above it all. When we boarded, there were only a handful of people sitting, and a few more clinging to the poles inside the train car to steady themselves. But the closer we got to Manhattan, the fuller the car became. By the time we dipped underground to pass underneath the East River, there were so many people I felt like I'd been shoved into a Poda Poda back home!

"We're going to hop off soon," Ibrahim said as the conductor began to mutter various Manhattan station names over the intercom.

"I'll follow you," I told him.

We stepped off at the 42nd Street station, and climbed a long set of grimy stairs out into the bright, New York sunshine. After walking a couple of blocks, we arrived at Times Square, and my jaw dropped.

Cars and taxis streamed by on the intersecting streets, and a massive Coca-Cola billboard flashed white and red above me. I saw half a dozen cinemas within a few blocks, and several strip clubs and burlesque bars. (Times Square has changed a lot since the 1970s!) Hundreds of people shuffled by us on the sidewalks, heads down, while car horns blasted at us from all sides. It was overwhelming…but also a little magical.

I caught Ibrahim grinning at me.

"What?" I said.

"New kid in the big city," he teased. I cuffed him on the shoulder. "Come on new kid, we're walking to Madison Square Garden."

I had never heard of this place before and had no idea what it was but followed my friend eagerly. We walked south down 7th Avenue until we hit 34th Street and found the Garden. The round, low building looked out of place among the towering skyscrapers but was still an amazing sight. Ibrahim explained that it was a sports arena, and I marveled that Americans could play their sports indoors!

After half an hour or so, we hopped on another subway to downtown Brooklyn so we could check that borough off our list. We didn't look around much, just peeked our heads out at the Fulton Street station.

Next we shot back over to lower Manhattan, where Ibrahim told me we'd get our lunch.

"There's this Greek restaurant on the east side at Delancey Street," he said. "They sell a sandwich called 'souvlaki,' a folded flatbread filled with lamb meat. It's my favorite. I want you to try it."

We hopped off the train at Delancey Street and I followed Ibrahim as he led me toward the restaurant. It was a small storefront, but big, mouthwatering smells were floating out from it. Ibrahim ordered for both of us, and we sat at a tiny table enjoying our souvlaki.

This was my first meal in America that hadn't been cooked at home by my friend, and I savored it. In fact, just like Ibrahim, souvlaki became my favorite sandwich in all of New York. (Even now when I go back to visit, I try to make my way back to that Greek restaurant on Delancey!)

After we'd eaten our fill, we ended up at South Ferry, where we boarded the Staten Island Ferry. As the boat left the terminal, the captain swung it near Liberty Island, giving me my first close view of the Statue of Liberty.

I will never forget that day of sightseeing for as long as I live. I saw more fascinating sights and famous places in that single day than I had seen in my entire life back in

Sierra Leone. It was a blessing and a dream come true for me to actually be in America, finally, after so many years of waiting and striving and hoping. I could hardly believe it was all real, and that I was finally there in person to experience it.

As we walked the streets of Manhattan and zipped through the dark subway tunnels, I thought about my mother and my departed father, wishing I could somehow share these experiences with them. I thought about the brothers and sisters that I had left behind in the village, how they'd likely never see any of these wonders in person themselves. Since I knew that words alone could never fully express all I had seen in New York, I asked Ibrahim to take pictures of me as we explored the city so I could mail them to my family back home.

When we finally returned home, the two of us spent the rest of the evening talking about things from our pasts. We reminisced about our primary and secondary school days in Sierra Leone and how we used to play soccer in the streets and local parks. It's funny how important it became to talk about home after seeing the thrilling sights all across New York. I was so enthralled by it all, but also a little bowled over. It was a relief to be back in the quiet of Queens with an old friend, and let my mind wander back to my homeland. I wasn't homesick—not even a little—but I needed to root myself in a few memories of Sierra Leone to gain my balance.

The Monday that followed our sightseeing excursion was also an unforgettable day…but for very different reasons. I'll always remember it as one of my very worst days in America.

That morning—about an hour after Ibrahim Wurie left the house—I decided to go for a train ride. I knew this would be a little bit risky since I was so new to America, but I thought it was the right thing to do. I wanted to try it not only for fun, but also for the sake of learning to navigate the subway system on my own. I walked to the Hillside Avenue subway station in Queens where I purchased a token for twenty-five cents and boarded the E-train bound for Manhattan, just as I'd done with Ibrahim on Saturday.

What followed was the longest train ride of my life.

When the E-train arrived at 42nd Street station, I recognized it as the Times Square stop and exited with a large group of passengers. So far so good. I headed up a staircase, then down another and hopped on another subway even though I had no idea where that train was going. Soon I found myself riding one train after another. I tried my best to decipher the subway maps on the platforms but was completely disoriented by being underground. Most of the larger subway stations are connected to each other by long walking tunnels, so I never even came up from underground. My adventure had become a fiasco.

Although I was somewhat concerned about becoming lost in the tangle of the subway system, I was not scared. However, I'd left home at 7 a.m. and when I saw that it was already 3 p.m. I decided eight hours of riding in the subway without a definite destination was enough.

I wanted to ask someone how to get back to Queens, but I was too intimidated. Everyone walked so quickly and looked so absorbed in their tasks, I didn't want to interrupt. And I certainly didn't want to aggravate anyone, or stumble over my English. But I realized at some point that I had to stop being bashful and talk to someone about my situation.

That point came when the train I was riding stopped and a New York City transit authority police officer entered the train and stood by the automatic doors. I immediately walked up to the officer and was bold enough to explain to him about my eight-hour ordeal in the subway. He responded to me with compassion and regret for the time I had been underground.

"I'm sorry to hear you've been stuck down here for so long," he said with real compassion. "Let me help you get back to Queens."

When the train we were riding arrived at the next station, the officer asked me to exit with him and we changed to another subway line. We went three stops and exited again. On that third stop, the officer finally got me onboard an E-train which would take me back to the Hillside Avenue station.

As I emerged into the afternoon light in Queens, I heaved a sigh of relief. I knew where I was, and I knew how to get home. I was exhausted as I walked slowly toward Ibrahim's house.

Shortly after I arrived, Ibrahim Wurie returned home from work. I told him all about my day, bravely battling the subway system.

"Oh, new kid," he said laughing, "you tried to do too much too soon!"

"I know," I mumbled. I was embarrassed but starting to see the humor in the situation, too.

"Always the ambitious one. Well, consider it a learning experience."

"And what was my lesson?" I asked.

"The subway can take you anywhere and everywhere…but it can also take you nowhere!"

Sightseeing and Touring NYC, 1972

Sightseeing and Touring NYC, 1972

Chapter 12

A Rough Start

Looking back, I realize exactly how fortunate I was to come to America in the way that I did. I'd been so eager to make my way across the ocean that I was prepared to do it all on my own. I could have arrived in New York or California speaking English and full of enthusiasm, but knowing no one and completely unprepared to acclimate to this new land. Instead, Ibrahim arrived first, became familiar with American life and culture, and acted as my guide. He eased me into this new life, and helped me figure out how to handle situations that otherwise might have totally overwhelmed me. He was my bridge between Sierra Leone and America, explaining and helping and preparing me slowly and patiently for my new life.

And yet, he couldn't stay with me every hour of every day. He had his own life, classes, and work to attend to. So I still encountered many stumbling blocks in those first months in New York.

The first was communication.

Once I began attending classes at RCA Institute and began to deal with the students, faculty, staff, and the general public on my own, I began to see my limitations.

Although I understood and spoke English fluently, I found that I had difficulty understanding many Americans and they had difficulty understanding me. I was asked many times to repeat myself when I spoke and, in turn, had to ask others to speak more slowly. To my ear they all spoke so quickly the words became a blur, and the heavy accents of Brooklyn and Long Island only made matters worse. To them, my speaking cadence and accent muddied the waters. Everyone was frustrated, and communication was slow.

However, as I continued to collaborate and interact with people in public, at the grocery store, and at school, I slowly began to understand more and communicate better. I gained confidence and started to relax a bit, which helped matters considerably. It turned out that my nervousness was tripping me up almost as much as my accent!

But let me rewind a bit and tell you about my first day of school…in America.

That day had some significant similarities *and* differences to my first day of school back in Sierra Leone. I arrived at RCA Institute feeling a bit bashful and overwhelmed, knowing myself to be an inexperienced freshman in a giant school teeming with students. But this time, I didn't let my nerves get the better of me. I didn't freeze up or refuse to speak or avert my eyes shyly. In fact, as I walked through the campus searching for my first classroom, I felt a surge of pride. I was excited to be among the diverse students at RCA, and knew that my presence in America was due to hard work and mindful accomplishment. I let my confidence guide me on that first day, and in the days to come.

I'd registered through the Department of Liberal Arts without a declared degree, and my first three classes were English 101, Chemistry 101, and Calculus 101. I had been an eager and excellent mathematics student during secondary school, and calculus was my very first class. Unfortunately, the instructor talked extremely fast and tended to explain concepts in a complicated way. As I sat through my first college course, my confidence began to waver. Maybe my English comprehension *wasn't* good enough. Would I feel this lost every day during my classes?

Back at home in Queens, I reviewed the material we'd covered that day in class and found I understood it perfectly. Alone with my textbook, I was able to grasp everything. But following and understanding the instructor would prove to be challenging all semester long.

As time went by, I tried harder to speak like an American. I wanted my own patterns of speech to shift, to sound more and more like a native. Whenever I had a conversation with someone, I paid close attention to what he or she said, taking mental notes about pronunciation and slang. When I spoke, I tried to put my observations to work and found that doing so made communication much, much easier. I might never pass for a real New Yorker, but after a few months I didn't sound quite so much like a brand new immigrant.

As my brain adjusted to communicating in new ways and navigating around on the subway, I was also acclimating to weather on the East Coast of America. When I'd arrived in May it had been cool and pleasant. Then came a long, hot, humid summer, which felt like a visit from an old friend. The real shock came once fall flew by and winter arrived.

I had never seen snow in my life.

I had no way to prepare for this strange new form of weather. I'd grown up dealing with rain during the rainy season, heat during the dry season, and high daily temperatures and humidity. We had hot days and cooler nights, but nothing that could be described as truly cold. Freezing temperatures, ice storms, and blizzards literally never happened in Sierra Leone. The first time I saw snowflakes falling outside my window I thought I was dreaming…until I realized I was not even sleeping!

My first winter in the U.S. was a challenging one. The ice and snow fascinated me, but I didn't understand how dangerous they could be. One day while I was in Manhattan, a snowstorm blew in and dropped six inches of snow on the ground. Totally unprepared, I'd worn a tee shirt, pants, and dress shoes that day. When I'd left the house that morning, it had been cool and sunny and my clothing choices had made perfect sense. The sudden temperature shift caught me off guard. I hadn't even purchased a winter coat, boots, or gloves yet, though Ibrahim had generously offered to let me borrow any of his own winter coats and clothes. I suffered miserably all day, convinced I would freeze to death.

Another time I was in class at the RCA Institute when all of the students were told we'd be dismissed early due to an incoming storm. After being let out of class, instead of proceeding to the subway and going home, I decided to roam around the city. I was underdressed for the weather yet again, but still excited to explore my new environment, and didn't feel ready to go back home. I walked around

Manhattan on my own, enchanted with my surroundings but gradually getting colder and colder. Within an hour, snow started falling and accumulated quickly. When I finally decided it was time to catch a train home, I started to descend into the subway station and fell down ten steps because they were so slippery. I must've gotten a concussion, because after the fall I lost feeling in several parts of my body. I thought my fingers, toes, and both ears had fallen off since I couldn't feel any of them. But I headed home, drank some hot tea, and wrapped myself in a thick blanket. Ibrahim shook his head at my foolishness, but also turned up the thermostat in the house to warm me. Within an hour, I was fine.

After those two incidents, I finally did what I should've done weeks before: Went shopping for cold weather clothes and a proper coat. Some people adapt easily to different types of climates, but I am not one of them. I never truly got used to living in a climate with freezing cold, snowy winters.

While my body was attempting to adjust to the weather, my insides were doing their best to get used to American food. This was strange and difficult in different ways. I'd never seen or eaten hamburgers, French fries, and hot dogs. In Sierra Leone, I was more likely to eat rice or fufu with cassava leaf, tola, and okra soup with palm oil or coconut oil in it. Breakfast or lunch might be cassava or boiled plantain with a touch of palm oil or honey. We woke up to lemon grass tea for an eye-opener. There was very little meat, no processed bread, and we prepared everything in ways that would seem strange to most American cooks.

Fast food restaurants were especially intimidating at first. Whenever I went to McDonald's or Burger King, I spent most of my time reading the menu behind the counter and trying my best to understand what the items were. Big Macs and Whoppers didn't sound like sandwiches, and so many foods had names that were more clever than descriptive. Sometimes I ordered the first thing that caught my eye to avoid holding up the line.

The only food I had no trouble adjusting to? Fried chicken. It looked and tasted familiar and having constant access to it at affordable prices was thrilling. In Sierra Leone, chicken is not for daily eating. Most households only prepare chicken on special occasions, when guests came for dinner or at a wedding celebration. Chickens are abundant both in the cities and villages of my home country, but we didn't consume them nearly as often as Americans.

And even though I'd seen images of New York City in books and movies, walking among the tall buildings felt strange and exciting. I used to bend my head backwards in order to get a good view of the skyscrapers. Although we had multi-story buildings in Freetown, they looked nothing like these giants. And I was used to crowded, bustling city streets, but midtown Manhattan, especially around Times Square, was constantly crowded, day and night. And the crowds were quite different from Freetown crowds: The people flooding Times Square tended to keep to themselves, snapping photos and staying out of each other's way. In Sierra Leone, city crowds were unbearably loud, and everyone stuck their nose into everyone else's business! The images of New York I'd absorbed so eagerly while daydreaming back in Sierra Leone turned out to be quite different from the reality of the city. In person, it was so much more lively and vibrant, the buildings were so impossibly tall. I fell in love with it all over again.

It was a lot to get used to, but I was more happy than overwhelmed. I was living my dream, studying in New York, the biggest city in America. I knew just how lucky I was.

But then my luck changed.

Just as I was starting to gain stability in America, I became the victim of mistaken identity.

After I'd attended two semesters at RCA Institute of Technology, I decided to transfer to New York City Community College (NYCC) in Brooklyn, where I took both day and night classes. I made this change because, after a year of living with Ibrahim in Queens, I had relocated to Brooklyn myself.

Ibrahim's nephew had moved in with the both of us, and although he was happy enough to sleep on the couch while we took the bedrooms, the house began to feel a bit crowded. As it happened, another friend of mine from Sierra Leone, Abu Bakarr Jalloh, had been living in Brooklyn but was moving to Michigan and needed someone to sublet his one-bedroom apartment. (Back in 1973, rent for that place was only $120 per month. Hard to believe!) When he asked if I was interested, my answer was a resounding "yes." Ibrahim was sad, saying he'd had big plans to find a larger house for all three of us to live in comfortably together, but I encouraged him to stay put. The Queens house had come to him through the kindness of a wonderful family, and his rent was incredibly affordable. So we parted ways, promising to spend as much weekend time together as possible now that we'd be living apart.

Shortly after I moved to Brooklyn, I began to ponder transferring schools. RCA was a long train ride away, while NYCC was just two subway stops from my new apartment. It didn't take long to realize that the shorter commute—and the ability to take evening classes at NYCC—were important advantages. So I made the switch.

One evening I left home, headed for the NYCC campus in downtown Brooklyn to take a night class. I was carrying a briefcase full of books. As I was walking down the subway steps to catch my train, I heard a loud gunshot. I stood there for a minute and heard two to three more rounds ring out through the echoing subway station.

Fear kicked in and I took off running up the stairway. I had no idea what was going on down there, and decided my best course of action was to get away from the sounds of shooting. I made it up the stairs and started running away from the entrance when two police officers ordered me to stop. Immediately, they both drew and pointed their guns at me. One of the officers told me to set my briefcase down and lay face-down on the ground. I followed his orders and down on the ground I went, stretching both arms out as I lay on my stomach face-down. The other officer walked over to where I lay, pulled both of my arms behind my back, and handcuffed me. After I was handcuffed they both pulled me up and walked me to their patrol car. One of them opened the back door and the other officer pushed me inside. Both officers got in the front and drove me to a precinct in Brooklyn. I was too scared to speak…but also knew that I was innocent and hoped that the truth would prevail in the end.

When we arrived at the precinct, they immediately took me to a room for questioning. The room was only about 12' by 16', with a small table and two chairs set opposite each other. They put me in one chair, and one of the officers sat in the other.

"What were you doing in that subway?" he asked gruffly. "And why did you run from us?"

"I was on my way to the NYCC campus for one of my night classes when I heard the sound of gunshots. So I ran. I didn't want to get hurt or shot."

He looked skeptical at my answer and continued to grill me about who I was, where I was going, how I'd come to New York, and more. I tried to explain that I was a foreign student here on a visa, studying in Brooklyn.

"What's in the briefcase?" one of them asked, tapping my bag with his pencil.

"Just books," I said.

"Open it up."

I did. And, as promised, it held nothing but my school books and papers.

But the interrogation dragged on. The two officers asked me dozens of questions which I answered truthfully, but they clearly didn't believe my story. They were preparing to lock me up when two *other* officers arrived at the precinct, with the actual subway shooter in custody. One popped his head into the interrogation room.

"We got him," was all he said.

The two officers who had arrested me apologized and set me free. They offered to take me to school, but since they'd already made me incredibly late to my night class, I declined their offer and told them I preferred to walk home alone. As a victim of mistaken identity, I expected much more from the police department, but all they offered me was a ride to school and an apology.

They did not realize the reason I was running was not because I committed a crime but I was running for my life. Fleeing from gunshots was an instinct that had carried over from my years in Sierra Leone. I had heard that sound so often during the years of political unrest, and had been conditioned to get as far away from it as I could, as fast as my legs could carry me. I'm not sure I could've stopped myself from running, even if I'd tried.

After I had lived in New York City and gone to school for a while, I realized it was time to find work. The cost of living was high and, although I was still receiving financial aid from my brother Abu, I did not have enough support to meet my daily needs. When I'd been living with Ibrahim, he had never directly asked for any rent money, but I'd always pitched in for both rent and household expenses. Now that I was living on my own, my cost of living had increased quite a bit. And since I was doing night classes at NYCC, I had my days free to work and start earning a bit more on my own.

As a foreign student, I had to request permission from Immigration and Naturalization to work. If the request was granted, it was understood that I could only work part-time. With that in mind, I went to the INS office in Manhattan and applied for a work permit. They asked for proof that I was attending school, which I had from the administration office of NYCC, so I was granted a work permit that same day.

An important first step, but just the first in many steps toward employment.

Luckily, finding a job in New York City in the mid-1970s was not nearly as difficult as it might be today. The day after the INS authorized me to work part-time, I picked up the New York Times and picked out several part-time and full-time jobs that sounded interesting to me. I made a phone call to a discount store in Manhattan to inquire about a part-time position, and was told to report for an interview that same day.

The interview was quite short, and I was not asked about my past work experience at all. The store manager simply explained the work duties, which mostly consisted of stacking merchandise on the shelves and replenishing items when they ran low. After the interview he hired me for the job, and my starting pay was $1.85 per hour. This pay rate was about average at the time. To give you some context, my rent was $120 per month, groceries typically cost about $20 per week, and subway fare was just $0.25. At $1.85 per hour, I wouldn't be able to live like a king, but with some supplementary support from my brother, I could make it work.

Working at the discount store was a learning experience. I would never say that I enjoyed the work, but it provided me with skills and training that would prepare me to be a valuable and reliable employee at my future jobs. The best thing about my position was that my schedule was "open," which meant I could report for work any time of the day once I was done with my day classes. I was expected to work Monday through Friday, but also typically put in a few hours on Saturdays, too. I was expected to work between 30 and 35 hours each week, and never failed to meet that quota. My boss valued my diligence and strong work ethic.

I didn't form any close friendships with my coworkers, but there were a handful who were friendly and welcoming. Some even showed me the most efficient ways to stock the shelves, helping me become a more efficient team player. There were a couple of guys who didn't seem to like me much, so I avoided and ignored them. I didn't want trouble, so I steered clear of confrontation. Eventually, the whole staff warmed to me. Everyone was especially cheerful on Fridays when our paychecks came. We'd all walk the two blocks down from the store to cash our checks together at a nearby bank, then get our lunch at a local restaurant as a big, jolly group.

About five months after I started working, my health took a turn. I woke up one day with a severe headache and fever, so I called in to say I couldn't work and didn't even try to attend my classes. Throughout that day, I had a burning sensation all over my body and by the next day I was having difficulty swallowing. My neck was stiff when I turned it and severe body aches set in.

Alarmed, I went to the emergency room of French Polyclinic Hospital in Manhattan. After several tests, I was referred to an ear, nose, and throat specialist who concluded that I was suffering from tonsillitis. He told me the mass of lymphoid tissue in my throat was so inflamed that it must be surgically removed.

Two days after the diagnosis I underwent a tonsillectomy. My job and schooling came to a temporary halt until I was fully recovered.

Before this setback, I'd been gaining confidence about the life I was building for myself in America. School was going well, I had a steady job, and I felt like I was finally settling in. This unexpected illness was a major setback, and I felt a little discouraged.

But looking back, I realized I had always experienced more downs than ups, and that my ability to rebound from difficult situations had always been my greatest strength. The surgery and recovery may have slowed me down temporarily, but I reacted with a renewed sense of hope for the future. I envisioned the wall between success and failure as a wall of glass; something that can be seen through, and something that can be shattered with courage and willpower. I knew success was still within my grasp, if I could just persevere.

And I did.

Chapter 13

Love Finds Me

It took me six long weeks to heal from my surgery, but once I was recovered I felt reinvigorated. Being forced to rest had given me time to consider how far I'd come, but also how far I still wanted to go. My desire to create a lasting and successful life for myself in the United States was stronger than ever before, and I began to consider my options.

I wasn't certain that NYCC was the best fit for me and was curious to know what it might be like to live outside of New York. I also knew that tuition to all of the colleges in the New York area was quite high, and I might be able to get a high quality education for less if I moved elsewhere. It was the fall of 1976 and I'd been in the U.S. for a little more than four years. My first best friend from school, Abdulai Sesay, had made the journey from Sierra Leone to New York a few months back, and was sharing the Brooklyn apartment with me, so I felt happy and well-established. My English was quite good at this point, I felt comfortable communicating and navigating. I had built a new life for myself and made many solid connections, but still had a few more semesters to complete my pre-med program and wondered if I could take my remaining courses somewhere less costly.

With that in mind, I gathered information about affordable tuition at Bay College of Maryland in Baltimore. I'd heard great things about both the city and the school from one of my relatives, Issa Bangura. Issa was the nephew of Shek Kabir, my sister Fatmata's husband, and he'd been living in Hyattsville, Maryland, while I was living and studying in New York. When I mentioned my quest to find a more affordable school, he recommended looking into Bay College as an alternative to NYCC. Soon afterwards, I found out that the college was offering financial aid and scholarships to qualified students and forwarded my transcripts as quickly as I could. Just three weeks later, the college wrote to offer me both admission and a partial scholarship that would cover my remaining time before graduation. With Issa's assistance I was able to transfer from New York to Hyattsville, Maryland, and continue my education at Bay College.

Just as Abu Bakarr Jalloh had generously offered me his Brooklyn apartment, Issa offered to let me move in with him. I was so grateful to have a fully furnished room to move into in Hyattsville and decided to pay that kindness forward to another Sierra Leonean. I asked my landlord to sign over the Brooklyn apartment to Abdulai and left him all of the furniture and kitchen items that Abu Bakarr had left to me.

But before I moved out of New York City, I wanted to learn how to drive.

The Baltimore area, where I'd be moving, didn't have a subway system and all my research told me that the best way to get around was by car. I was talking about this with a friend, Alex Kamara, and he immediately offered to teach me how to drive.

"It will be fun!" he said. "But before we get started, we need to get you a learner's permit."

I spent two whole days studying my heart out for the written exam, then headed down to the Department of Motor Vehicles to take the test. I passed with flying colors, and Alex told me it was time to get behind the wheel.

Most of our lessons were in quiet parks and dead-end streets, places where there weren't too many other cars or active pedestrians to get in my way. Alex was a rigorous instructor, who told me I should be practicing at least two hours each day, and longer on weekends. After a month of this, I felt ready to take my road test. Alex agreed I had all the skills I needed, and had taken to driving like a natural. He scheduled my road test, accompanied me to the DMV, and cheered when I passed. Within a week, I had my driver's license.

My next step, of course, was to get a car.

Back in Sierra Leone, I'd been fascinated by people who owned cars. As a child, that level of luxury and independence seemed so far out of reach, but I secretly hoped one day I might be a car-owner myself. An older couple out on Long Island made my hopes come to fruition.

Shortly after I'd secured my license, I saw a classified ad for a 1967 Chevy Impala that was within my price range. The elderly couple was eager to find it a good home, so Alex and I headed out to test drive it as soon as we could. I loved the car and bought it on the spot. That same day, they signed ownership over to me and I drove my very first car back to

Brooklyn. It was a proud day for me, another long-time dream fulfilled in America.

That car took me and my handful of belongings from New York down to Maryland in just a few hours. As I drove away from my first home in America, I felt a little sadness, but also excited to begin a new chapter in my new life here.

I stayed with Issa and his wife in their Hyattsville apartment for two months, and they spent that time showing me around the area. Shortly after that, Issa's younger brother, Santigie, suggested that he and I get our own apartment together. Issa's wife was pregnant, and he needed his spare room back! Santigie was also attending Bay College, and we rented a two-bedroom apartment together in a complex that also housed other students.

Soon after I began attending classes, I noticed that the college was committed to serving its students by providing convenient, comprehensive and diverse educational experiences. Bay College also had some really excellent support services, including a carpooling program, which I used quite often. Santigie and I lived more than 30 miles from campus, so carpooling into Baltimore was a life-saver.

Graduation from Bay College of Maryland, 1977

After two consecutive semesters of a grade average of As and Bs, I made the Dean's List for scholastic excellence. In May of 1977 I graduated from Bay College and in the fall of that year, I enrolled at the University of Baltimore to continue my education.

Nineteen seventy-seven was also the year that I met the woman I would later marry. And, oddly enough, our first encounter was at an award ceremony.

After moving to Hyattsville, I'd joined a group called "Sakoma," a Temene word that means, "We are from the same family." Sakoma was founded by students from Sierra Leone living in the Washington D.C. metropolitan area, and its purpose was to give us a support network of other expatriates who understood our common cultural experiences. The support was mainly social, but also financial; if a member was getting married or had a death in the family, the group contributed money to offset the costs. I loved participating in Sakoma. It made me feel like I could keep a little piece of Sierra Leone with me everywhere I went. I became deeply involved in the group and was organizing secretary from 1977 to 1978.

Sakoma members were asked to write articles on various subjects, describing their experiences with and revelations about life in America, and the best of them were published in the group's magazine. I wrote an article about marriages and the reasons people choose to marry which was chosen for publication, and the fateful award ceremony was celebrating those of us who'd been featured in the magazine.

I will never forget that night, since it was a huge turning point in my life. I'd worn black dress pants and a white, short-sleeved shirt with a pineapple design on the front left side and was feeling very neat. As I made my way around the room, I spotted a woman in a blue and black dress that had sheer detailing on the sleeves and around the hem. She smiled shyly when she caught my eye, then looked away.

I'm not sure what she was feeling at that moment but for me, it was love at first sight.

As the evening progressed, I knew I needed to make a move. The event was full of vibrant energy and everyone in attendance was enjoying themselves. The DJ was playing upbeat dance music, and everyone was on the dance floor having a blast. But the woman in the blue and black dress was sitting off to the side with two other girls—who I soon discovered were her sisters—seemingly waiting for an invitation. This was my chance.

I walked over to them, and got right to the point.

"Miss, I was wondering if you might like to dance with me," I said, trying to sound as confident as possible.

She smiled slowly and said, "Sure."

I offered her my hand, she stood up, and we walked to the dance floor just as a slow song came on.

"My name is Ansu," I said as I placed my hands on her shoulder and waist.

"I'm Evelyn," she told me quietly.

"I hope you don't mind me saying this, but you are far and away the most beautiful girl here tonight."

She laughed, a light twinkly sound, and smiled up at me. "Well, thank you," she replied.

It might not have been the most creative opening line, but it certainly let her know my intentions. And soon we were chatting away about our lives and dreams. I told her I was studying in Baltimore but originally from Sierra Leone, and she lit up.

"Really? How fascinating," she said. "Once I've finished my schooling, I've always imagined joining the

Peace Corps and working in Africa. I've dreamed about it for ages."

The more we talked, the more we became enraptured with one another. She told me she lived in Texas and was visiting Maryland with her sisters. I told her I had recently moved here from New York, where I'd studied in Manhattan. Sparks were flying, and before the song had ended I had asked if I could call her once in a while, and she'd promised to give me her number before the night was through.

We chatted for a few minutes after the dance was over, then drifted apart, but we watched each other from across the room the whole night. I could tell that my fate was wrapped up in this lovely woman.

This was a new feeling for me. During my school days in Sierra Leone, I'd met plenty of pretty girls, many of whom had expressed a desire to date me, even possibly marry me. But none of them ever really caught my eye, and I'd never really been in love. I was too focused on my education to be bothered with something as frivolous as romance, and worried that if I became involved with any women in Sierra Leone, it might derail my plans to relocate to America. I'd played it safe, and mostly kept away from dating.

But meeting Evelyn felt entirely different. I was already in America, well on my way to achieving my dreams, and she'd entered my life when my heart was open. Meeting her felt fateful, destined, and very, very exciting. Even though she lived halfway across the country, I knew we would find a way to make it work.

And we did.

A few days after we met, Evelyn returned to Kilgore, Texas. We started corresponding by mail and talking on the telephone, eagerly sharing everything about our pasts and presents and dreaming together about our futures. The more we got to know each other, the more we realized we belonged together. We fell in love in absentia. Within six months, I knew I never wanted to be without her.

I decided to make a traditional proposal by first explaining my intent to her parents, Mr. and Mrs. Williams. I also wanted to ask Evelyn for her hand in marriage in person with her parents present. With their approval, I caught a flight from Maryland to Texas. Evelyn's family was incredibly welcoming to me; I had planned to stay in a motel in downtown Kilgore, but they insisted I stay in their guest room. Once I'd arrived, I took them aside and explained my plan. They told me that if their daughter wanted to spend her life with me, they'd stand behind her decision.

Later that day, we had a small, informal gathering at the Williams's home. Her parents invited some of her aunts, uncles, and cousins to join us, and prepared an amazing feast. Mr. Williams was a renowned barbecue cook, and everyone in attendance was excited, happy, and well-fed.

Once the initial excitement had died down a little and folks had gotten a chance to eat, I made a short speech and asked for Evelyn's parents' blessing on our engagement. There were tears and applause and much joy. Evelyn herself absolutely radiated happiness as I spoke about my ever-growing love for her, and promised to keep her safe and build a marvelous life together. I had brought a ring with me from Maryland, and when I placed it on her finger, I felt a deep satisfaction well up within me. Evelyn placed her small hand on my cheek, and as we shared a kiss, her whole family cheered.

Not long after that, we went back to Maryland to begin our life together.

Instead of flying, we decided to take a Greyhound Bus. Evelyn suggested this because it was much cheaper, and would give me the chance to glimpse many cities and states that I'd never visited. It was an extremely long bus ride—48 hours from Texas to Maryland—but we had a fantastic time looking at the scenery and getting to know each other even better. During the day, we watched the scenery fly by and Evelyn told me bits and pieces of American history. At night, when all was darkness, we talked about our hopes and dreams. The bus passed through Shreveport, Louisiana; Jackson, Mississippi; Birmingham, Alabama; Atlanta, Georgia; Jacksonville, South Carolina; Greensboro, North Carolina; Richmond, Virginia and Washington, D.C. In addition to these cities, we saw massive cotton fields dotted with white, smelled the rich fragrances of tobacco plantations, and endless rows of corn.

About two months before I traveled to Texas to propose to Evelyn, I had parted ways with my roommate and rented my own apartment in the same complex. So when we arrived in Maryland together, we had a place all to ourselves. Although it was most common at this time for people to marry before living together, our circumstances were such that we needed to take those steps in reverse. None of her family objected, as we'd waited to become formally engaged before combining our households, and our wedding was already being planned. As we lived together and made preparations for our life as husband and wife, we built our relationship brick by brick until we stood on a solid foundation. We learned more about each other, came to appreciate each other's strengths and learned to accommodate each other's quirks. Over the months, we fell deeper in love, while also cultivating trust, cooperation, and mutual support, until we decided we were ready for matrimony.

Shortly after we moved in together, Evelyn started looking for work. In short order, she was hired at a mailing company that had offices not far from our apartment complex. I was still in school at the time, so I attended classes while she worked.

On July 19, 1978, family members from Texas and Maryland and friends and neighbors witnessed our exchange of vows at the Upper Marlboro courthouse in Maryland. My close family was still in Sierra Leone and unable to attend, but a few distant relatives and many friends I'd made in America joined us for the ceremony. I was delighted to see Ibrahim among them! Evelyn's family was huge, and many of them made the journey to the East Coast to witness our union. A justice of the peace conducted the ceremony and pronounced us husband and wife.

Afterwards, a hired driver was meant to pick up me and my new wife, take us back to our apartment to change our clothes, then swing back shortly and take us to the reception site. We swapped our wedding clothes for our reception clothes fairly quickly...but the driver was nowhere in sight. Minutes ticked by, and turned to nearly an hour.

"Where could he be?" Evelyn exclaimed, anxious and upset. "I'm sweating through my reception dress! I've got to take it off."

Flustered, she headed to the bedroom to cool off and wait. When the driver finally returned, she called to me.

"Ansu, could you help me with the laces on my dress, please?"

Her reception dress was a lovely but complex garment with laces up the back. I wanted to be helpful, but was so nervous that I fumbled with the interlocking strings and took forever to get it right. I could tell she was doing her best to be patient but was gradually becoming more and more anxious.

"There, I think that does it," I finally said, now a little sweaty myself.

"Great. Now let's GO!" she said.

We hustled out the car together and zoomed over to the party.

We had a jubilant reception at an enormous banquet hall that the Sakoma organization had rented out on our behalf. Our very late arrival prompted many jokes and jabs from our guests, who'd be waiting patiently for us.

"So, you just couldn't wait for the honeymoon, eh?" people kept saying. We blushed and looked knowingly at each other. The truth was far less interesting, but also far more amusing to us.

Sakoma had also provided the food and drinks for all 100 attendees, since part of the group's mission was to support its members in life transitions. We received many gifts, as well as a generous cash gift from Sakoma, meant to help us launch our new life together. The party was one of the most joyous and memorable events of my life, and I can still hear the laughter and well-wishes ringing in my imagination.

Shortly after our wedding, my wife became pregnant. We were both thrilled at the idea of becoming parents so soon, but her pregnancy forced me to reconsider my own career plans. I had been continuing my education in hopes of eventually getting my medical degree and becoming a physician. With a baby on the way, however, I knew that going on to medical school would be risky. Where would I get the money to support my wife and baby? Was it selfish to keep studying when what my new family really needed was financial support?

I thought long and hard before reaching a decision but finally concluded that I needed to quit school and find a full-time job.

However, I made this decision without discussing it with Evelyn.

So one day, when I returned home from school and told her that I wouldn't be going back because I needed to seek permission to work full-time, she didn't believe me.

"You're not serious, Ansu," she said. "You love school! And you've always wanted to be a doctor. And I've always wanted to be a doctor's wife!"

"I know, and you're right," I said. "But our situation has changed. With the baby coming, we can't expect my scholarships and loans to support us all. It's just not enough money."

"Isn't there any other way?"

"Not that I can see," I told her.

But even then, she thought I was bluffing. She knew how much I loved learning and how passionate I was about getting a stellar education, and must've thought I'd realize I was being foolish and head back to classes.

The following day, when I did not leave for school, she actually wept.

The choice was hard on me, too. Evelyn and I had talked quite a bit about my intention to go back to Sierra Leone after I graduated from medical school. I wanted to be of service to the sick and suffering people in my own village, and to the citizens of Sierra Leone in general. I had considered this to be part of my destiny, my calling, for many years. My heart broke just a little bit as I was forced to let go of that vision of myself.

But I had always tried to make wise, informed decisions throughout my life. Some of those decisions had pleasant endings, others had been disappointing. Regardless of the results, my ultimate goal in decision-making was not just to benefit myself, but to benefit those I cared about, and the world in general whenever possible. Deep in my heart I wanted to continue my education, become a doctor as I'd always planned. But it would have been impractical and short-sighted to ignore the reality of my new wife and coming baby. I could put off my education, but there was no putting off the baby! And since I could not financially support my education and a family at the same time, I made a tough choice, but one that felt vital at the time.

Chapter 14

An Unexpected Turn in My
Career Path

Since I wanted to work full-time, I needed to become a permanent resident of the United States. The work permit that was issued to me in New York City was only for part-time employment, and I had no desire to risk breaking the law.

So Evelyn and I went to the U.S. Immigration Office in Baltimore and I applied for permanent resident status. After we handed over the required documents, we were told that my application would begin processing immediately, but that would take several months to make it through the entire system. I was still working part-time when I applied. After 90 days had passed, my wife and I attended a mandatory interview.

This interview was a fascinating and unique experience. The purpose of the interview was to confirm that I, the applicant, was really living with my wife, a natural U.S. citizen. They want to weed out anyone who has created a phony marriage for the purposes of securing a green card. To this end, they separated me from Evelyn, asked us both the same set of questions, and compared our answers. The questions were things like, "What did you eat for dinner last night?" and "What color is your spouse's toothbrush?", little mundane details that would prove we were truly partners and living together as husband and wife.

We passed the interview process with flying colors and afterwards I was issued a green card, which automatically changed my status from student to permanent resident.

By this time my wife was four months pregnant and counting.

My new status as a permanent resident made it fully legal for me to work and live in the United States, and I wasted no time tracking down a steady job. The work I found wasn't glamorous, but I was able to build upon it over the years and create a successful career for myself in an unexpected field.

In early 1979, I began my job search. I wanted to work somewhere close to home, so I drove around the Hyattsville area scoping out potential employers. A company called Graphic Fine Color, Inc., a printing ink manufacturing company, was just four miles from our apartment, and I saw that they were hiring. I decided to investigate.

When I entered the building, I went straight to the receptionist's desk and told her that I wanted to fill out an application for a job. The receptionist paged the operations manager. He was a portly man, only about five and a half feet tall, wearing khaki pants, a white shirt, and a tie. He introduced himself as Jim Cummins, and showed me to his office.

"Well, young man, the only position we have available just now is a janitor," he said.

"And what does a janitor do?" I asked.

"Mostly routine cleaning. Sweeping the offices, collecting the trash, mopping up the ink that spills onto the floor during daily plant operations."

"How much does it pay?"

"$4.25 an hour to start."

"When can I start?"

He chuckled a bit. "Well, tomorrow, if you're able!"

So on April 26, 1979, I began working at Graphic Fine Color as a janitor. The job market was tough at that time and I was desperate to work and willing to perform any job assignment. Also, our baby had arrived just a few weeks before, on April 15, and I wanted to support my new family. So even though the work wasn't challenging, I made every effort to do it well. Every day, after I clocked in, I vacuumed out the offices and emptied their trash cans. But most of my day was spent cleaning up after ink spills around the plant. Weighing ink materials was a fussy process, and several ink spills were expected every day. Those spills had to be dealt with right away to prevent workers from tracking ink from the manufacturing area into the offices. As the janitor, I was responsible for keeping the plant clean and tidy, and I took my responsibilities seriously.

My fastidiousness paid off. After six months, my manager told me he was impressed by my work ethic and positive attitude and wanted to promote me. I was moved to the varnish department, which also manufactured dispersions for water-based ink. It was in this department that my knowledge and experience in printing ink manufacturing began to grow, and my new career began to unfold.

On my first day in the varnish department, I trained under the manager in charge, learning the techniques of varnish manufacturing and dispersions, the type of varnishes, and quality control methods. Graphic Fine color was serious about quality control, and our processes included laboratory testing of finished products to meet specifications, as well as testing the raw materials including resins, gellant, and additives. I was a quick learner, and it wasn't long after I'd completed my basic training until I was able to get involved in the manufacturing operations. I was fascinated by the processes, and absorbed this new pool of knowledge quickly and eagerly. My coworkers recognized my growing understanding and trustworthiness. After a few months, I was a valued member of the varnish team. Whenever the manager in charge was on vacation or scheduled to be off, he chose me to oversee production in his absence.

From 1979 to 1984, I continued to model good workmanship in the varnish department and build my reputation as a team player. In 1985, the scheduling manager was assigned to another department and I was selected by upper management to coordinate the day-to-day production schedule of the varnish department. I was given management responsibilities, but no change in title; it was like a trial run to see how I would handle the new workload. This recognition enabled me to work directly with the operations manager, who oversaw all of the departments in the company.

Under the leadership of my predecessor, our maximum production on a regular workday was a total of 5,000 pounds of varnish. Once I was given the responsibility of coordinating the production schedule, I did my best to motivate and inspire all of the employees in my area. I encouraged them to work sensibly but harder, and was eventually able to double production from 5,000 pounds to 10,000 pounds per day.

Upper management recognized this achievement and its direct impact on the growth of the company. In mid-1985, I was promoted to varnish department manager.

This promotion secured me an invitation to the daily meetings attended by all of the company's departmental managers. The purpose of these meetings was to foster communication between the departments so that work flowed smoothly. This might sound like an awful lot of time dedicated to building interdepartmental camaraderie but it was essential. In printing ink manufacturing, all departments contribute to the completion of one can of ink, so good communication is crucial.

In 1988, Graphic Fine Color moved to a brand new 65,000 square foot state-of-the-art plant in Annapolis Junction, Maryland. Moving to the new facility required a new round of technical and manufacturing training, especially after the company invested in a new DRAIS mill to incinerate carbon black ink. Operating the DRAIS mill required knowledge of the mill and manufacturing skills.

To continue my growth with Graphic Fine Color, upper management decided it was in the best interest of the company for me and a member of the technical team to attend a few company-sponsored seminars. These seminars would help us understand the carbon black manufacturing process and train us in the basics of working the DRAIS mill.

We started at a chemical plant in Patterson, New Jersey, where we observed their manufacturing processes and received training from the best carbon black manufacturing personnel in the printing ink industry. Then we flew to Buffalo, New York, to a plant that used a totally different setup to create carbon black ink. Finally, we drove across Niagara Falls to our final destination, another printing ink manufacturing plant located in Toronto, Canada. We arrived in Toronto just before nightfall. We would spend an entire week observing and learning there.

During this period in Toronto, Canada, I not only observed the manufacturing process of carbon black ink, but participated in the process to have a feel of how things are actually done in that plant. I learned more about the operation of the DRAIS mill, pre-mix process, the flow of ink in and out of the mill, and the quality control of the finished product. That was the knowledge and information that I needed to take back with me to our plant.

A week later, our heads filled with new knowledge, we flew back to Maryland.

Shortly after my return, I started training the employees assigned to the carbon black department. Before long, each of them was able to operate the DRAIS mill and manufacture carbon black.

By 1990, I had been with the company for 11 years and my service record was dotted with many significant accomplishments. I continued to receive many service awards, my entire team was valued, and I was recognized as an effective and trusted leader. Upper management evaluated all of my efforts when they considered me for another promotion, and by the middle of 1990, I was assigned the duties of both varnish and carbon black manufacturing departments. Because of the additional assignment, I was elevated to the position of manufacturing manager.

The second promotion with Graphic Fine Color not only brightened my image with the company, but also drastically improved my family's financial status. I could never have imagined that a position as a janitor would lead to such a successful career when I had to quit school to support my family. I had strayed far from the path of a medical doctor, but found an engaging job with plenty of growth opportunity for myself in the process.

Ansu Kamara, manufacturing manager, Graphic Fine Color and Barry Nightingale, plant engineer, Canadian Fine Color

Ansu Kamara observing a double motor ink mixing tank at
Canadian Fine Color, Toronto

From L to R: Murray Scott, operations manager at Canadian
Fine Color; Ansu Kamara, manufacturing manager, Graphic
Fine Color and Bernard Denisar, technical manager, Graphic
Fine Color

Chapter 15

Achievements and Losses

After 13 years of permanent resident status with a "green card," I decided that it was time for me to become a U.S. citizen. It was 1992, and I now had a wife, two lovely children, a home, and a thriving career. I discussed my intention with my wife and children, and they all supported the decision.

So I began the legal process of applying for citizenship through the United States Immigration and Naturalization Service. From the date I submitted my application request, the entire process took one year. During that time, I was asked to present certain required documents, schedule an interview, and take a naturalization test. The test involved knowledge about the U.S. branches of government, the names and duties of certain government officials, and other general questions. I attended the interview on my scheduled date and successfully passed the test.

About one month after the interview, I received a letter from Immigration and Naturalization stating that I had been selected to participate in an outdoor naturalization ceremony. The ceremony was in honor of "I am An

American Day," and would be held at Patterson Park in Baltimore.

And so on September 12, 1993, along with nearly 200 other eager attendees, I took the oath of citizenship and became a U.S. citizen. It was a bright fall day, filled with sunshine and anticipation, and everyone who participated brimmed with hope. The park was decorated with many American flags, and filled with attendees singing patriotic music. A few tears were shed, but they were all tears of joy.

I am proud to be an American holding my
Certificate of Naturalization

As I walked up to the stage to receive my naturalization certificate, I was filled with deep pride and a sense of accomplishment. It had been a long road, with many twists and turns, but I had progressed slowly and steadily toward my goal. I was an American citizen, living in the country of my dreams. As my wife and children cheered me on, I was speechless with gratitude and joy.

Unfortunately, that joy was short-lived.

Shortly after the ceremony, I received heartbreaking news from my family in Sierra Leone. My mother was seriously ill and was not responding to medications. A doctor in Freetown had diagnosed her with a life-threatening heart condition.

I responded to the news by making emergency preparations to go to Sierra Leone, hoping I'd be able to bring Mother to the United States for emergency treatment. Just five days after I received the news, I left for Sierra Leone.

As soon as I arrived, I went straight to the U.S. embassy in Freetown and applied for a medical visa on behalf of my mother. They asked for basic documentation for the medical treatment visa, such as the diagnostic report, the status of the person making the request, and proof of accommodation and financial support. Since I had witnessed (and even helped) several friends bring their relatives to the United States from foreign countries, I was familiar with the procedure and already knew what would be needed. I went to the embassy fully prepared. Two days after I made the request, the process was completed. The embassy issued a multiple visa for my mother to travel to the United States for medical treatment. About three days after the visa was issued, my 76-year-old mother and I flew from Sierra Leone to Baltimore.

The day after we arrived in the U.S., my wife and I took my mother to the office of a cardiovascular disease specialist in Columbia, Maryland, where she underwent extensive diagnostic tests. The results showed she had high blood pressure and high cholesterol. The doctor recommended a change of diet and regular exercise. In addition, he prescribed blood pressure and cholesterol-lowering medications. We were relieved that she didn't need some sort of major surgery, but still worried about her condition. She was weak and not her usual lively self.

But with daily doses of the prescribed medications, regular exercise, and a healthy diet of non-fat foods improved her condition. About one month later, her blood pressure was normal and her cholesterol was under control. She was also taking high potency multivitamins, which gave her energy to do her exercise, daily walks around the neighborhood in the early evening.

Although her arrival had been under dire circumstances, my mother's time with us in America soon settled into a calm and happy routine. She had never met Evelyn or my children, and was absolutely elated to finally spend time with them. Of course, she only spoke Temene and my family only spoke English, so I had to spend a lot of time interpreting! While I was at work and the kids were at school, my mother and Evelyn worked out a kind of sign language so they could communicate in my absence. I was thrilled and fascinated to see this unfold.

My two kids were smart and rambunctious and had the time of their lives playing with their grandmother. They even pulled a few practical jokes on her, but all in good fun.

One Saturday morning, just after we had finished breakfast, the kids went down to the basement to hatch a plan. They tied a bunch of wadded up paper and some old balloons to a rope, and taped it all to the ceiling, but attached to a rope. Then, they hid behind the sofa holding the rope and started calling to their grandma.

"Come play with us, Grandma!" they hollered, giggling their mischievous little heads off.

My mother made her way down to the basement to find them. She immediately spotted the bizarre cluster of junk attached to the ceiling, but couldn't figure out why it was there, and kept searching for the kids. They waited until she was in just the right spot, yanked the rope, and brought the whole mess down on top of her! Then they scrambled out from their hiding spot, laughing uproariously, and grabbed at her. My mother knew all about practical jokes from growing up with me and my siblings, and laughed with them until her sides were sore.

My mother was also totally mesmerized by television, something she'd never experienced in Sierra Leone. It was a little tough to explain the concept to her, even when I tried in Temene, and she seemed to think that whatever she saw playing out on the screen was actually happening in real life!

One evening we were all gathered around the TV watching together. My two kids sat on either side of my mother, and came up with yet another trick. They'd noticed how riveted she was by everything happening on screen, and seemed to sense that she believed it was all real.

"Grandma, you need to fix your head tie and straighten yourself up," my daughter said. "The people on the TV are looking at you!"

I knew what was up, but translated anyway just to see what would happen. Sure enough, my mother began to retie her head scarf and straighten up her dress, so she'd look sharp for the characters on the screen.

We couldn't contain ourselves. The kids, Evelyn, and I all laughed so hard we rolled off the couch onto the floor.

After being in America for about eight months, even though she had multiple visas, Mother was ready to go back to Sierra Leone. I encouraged her to stay a bit longer but my efforts failed. She had enjoyed her time here but she preferred to be where she was more familiar with the surroundings and the way of life. Since she could not speak English and couldn't really navigate her way through an American airport alone, I had to take her back to Sierra Leone.

Before we left, I contacted my sister Fatmata in Freetown and let her know the details of our arrival. She passed this information along to the rest of the family in Robomp Bana, who all traveled to Lungi International airport to meet us. When we arrived back in Sierra Leone I stayed there for two weeks to ensure that Mother continued to improve and to spend time with my family, who were all gathered there. Then I told her to keep up with everything the doctor had ordered, said a sad farewell, and returned to the United States.

The medical treatment Mother received in the United States gave her four more years of good life. When she returned, she lived gracefully in good health through 1997, when she finally passed away.

I have several precious pictures of my mother, and every so often I look at them and think of her. Each time I do, those old photos bring back a flood of memories. Evelyn has asked several times if we could hang a few photos of my beloved mother around our house, but I just couldn't bring myself to do it. It's been decades since she passed away now, but it somehow feels like just yesterday, and seeing her image reminds me that she's truly gone. I save the photos for quiet moments alone when I can dive deep into my memories and allow my heart to miss her as deeply as it desires.

As for my father, I don't have any pictures of him and I don't believe anyone in my family does. I can only see my father in my mind's eye whenever thoughts of him come to mind.

Although I missed my parents and the loss of my mother left a hole in my heart forever, I have never been one to dwell in the past. I tried to focus on the present and think about how proud they would be as I continued to build a successful life for myself and my family in America.

I continued to achieve tremendous success at Graphic Fine Color and enjoyed my work there nearly every day. My determination to manufacture the best product that met the needs of our customers was above and beyond the normal standard. Part of the key to my success was being open to suggestions, especially when my employees were communicating their ideas, observations of problems, and suggestions for improvement. I spoke often about the importance of teamwork and I meant it; I encouraged everyone to be part of the team.

Every bit of work I did had a sense of urgency, both because our company had to manage a number of quick-turn orders and because I had a natural habit of getting things done on a timely basis. Whenever I received an order, I processed it with extreme urgency. That kind of performance was what set me apart from my peers. It was also the kind of performance that enabled upper management to easily recognize my untiring effort in contributing to the growth of the company.

I continued to be dependable and productive at Graphic Fine Color and upper management truly appreciated my efforts. They showed their appreciation, not only by words and pay increases, but by allowing me to expand my knowledge about printing ink manufacturing and other skills. My hungry mind always appreciated the opportunity to learn and gain and grow.

Chapter 16

Hope Was My Compass

After 20 years of continuous service with Graphic Fine Color and living happily in Maryland, my wife decided it was time for us to move to Texas. Her father had died of lung cancer and her mother was living alone at the family home, so Evelyn wanted to be close to her mother as she grew older.

Coincidentally, just as my wife came to this decision, I received a call about an available production manager position at Emerald Printing Inks, a company that manufactured water-based inks in San Antonio, Texas. Everything seemed to be coming together at once.

Allan King, the CEO of Emerald Inks and a friend of mine for many years, invited me to visit the plant in San Antonio and spend a week getting to know the area. During my visit, we discussed the position, job responsibilities, and salary. In addition, he offered me full family health benefits, a bonus plan, and a company-sponsored retirement plan. The offer was obviously good and I was thrilled to accept it.

Upon my return to Maryland, I sadly but respectfully resigned from Graphic Fine Color. I was given an honorary celebration and full pay for all my accumulated benefits. A luncheon was held on my behalf and I was given several gifts, which I deeply appreciated.

Then in August of 1999 my wife, three kids (we'd had another in the meantime), and I relocated to San Antonio where I would continue my career and Evelyn could look after her dear mother.

One of the benefits included in my hiring package was relocation assistance. Emerald hired a moving company to transfer all of our belongings to San Antonio, and I was also granted six months of storage for free. This gave us time to settle in. About a month before the move, I bought a brand new Chevy S10 Blazer and the whole family drove to Texas. We left Maryland on a Friday morning and arrived in San Antonio at around 3 a.m. on Sunday.

I knew I would miss the lively and welcoming culture of the East Coast. Living in Maryland for so long, I'd become accustomed to every celebration including a crab feast and loved the friendly openness of the residents. We spent many evenings crowding into basements to chat and catch up with our friends. People in the Baltimore area definitely know how to have fun.

But the weather in Maryland wasn't always fun. I never did get used to the cold, wet winters or heavy snow. In my 22 years living there, I witnessed snow and ice wreak havoc on the lives of all residents. I was more than happy to leave all that behind for a warmer climate.

As we settled into Texas, I noticed some similarities. There were no crab feasts, but barbecue took their place, making an appearance at virtually every party we attended. Most homes in Texas lack basements, and gatherings take place outside instead. Winters were wonderfully warm and mild, but summers were punishingly hot. I'd traded one kind of terrible weather for another!

I served Emerald Printing Inks to the best of my ability for nine years. In January 2008, after a combined total of 29 years in the same line of work, I decided to retire from the ink industry. I loved my work, but saw that the industry was changing. With new innovations like UV and soy-based inks, the water-based inks I'd produced my whole career were falling out of favor. Business began to taper off, and I knew it was time to make a change. Shortly after I'd reached this decision, Emerald lost a huge account that comprised 80% of our business, and I knew it was time.

I did, however, keep working in other fields. I spent time with Forum Oilfield Technologies, a company that manufactured pumps and valves for offshore and land drilling. I was a leadman for several departments and oversaw dozens of employees. At Dart Drug Warehouse II I worked as a forklift operator for a short period, before being promoted to foreman in charge of seasonal merchandise. I also worked for a company that manufactured car batteries, employed me as a quality control specialist. In addition, I am also the founder and president of Sierra Enterprise, a self-publishing and distribution company.

Today, my wife and I still live in San Antonio and enjoy our shared life here. Our three children have had five grandchildren, and although we don't see them quite as often as we'd like to, we cherish every moment we get with them. I feel extremely fortunate that my dream of carving out a life for myself in Sierra Leone became a reality. It took hard work, patience, cunning, and the ability to persevere in the face of enormous obstacles. And it took the support and love of the family and friends who saw my dream reflected in my young face, and did everything in their power to help me achieve it.

But most of all, it took hope. My undying optimism and refusal to be discouraged were the beacons that lit my way. Even when I was scared, ill, lost, or overwhelmed, my hope for a better future never faded. Without hope, I might never have come this far.

And as someone who has taken a long, winding journey of hope, I'd like to offer you, dear reader, some advice. No matter where you are in life or what your dreams may be, I hope my words will find their home in your heart and mind:

If you believe you can succeed and work patiently toward your goals, you can achieve virtually anything. I was born in a simple, undeveloped society in a nation where illiteracy was widespread. Sierra Leone offered limited opportunities and unlimited challenges. But despite the conditions in which I was born and raised, I was desperate and determined to succeed in life. And, slowly but surely, I did.

You cannot wish yourself into leadership, but if you work hard you can forge yourself into a strong and worthy leader. The fact that I rose through the rank and file from janitor to varnish department manager to manufacturing manager and then to production manager positions is proof that true effort and hard work pay off. I am living proof that America is a country where anything is possible.

Never say "never." Don't allow yourself to indulge in negative thinking. If you dwell in thoughts like *this is too difficult or tiresome or burdensome* or *I'm not cut out for this kind of work*, you will make that negativity into reality. Hold tight to your optimism, and never let go.

Be open to happiness, and welcome success. If you want this life to deliver to you all of the things you have been wishing for—prosperity, a fine home, financial security, leadership—you must open yourself to their arrival. Look for the tools you can use to create a path to your desired achievements.

When you believe you can do something, you allow the knowledge, power, skill, and energy required to develop inside you. The power of belief is neither mystical nor magical. You can create your own success by first believing you can succeed, and then following the path to achieve your goal.

Trust hope. Let it guide you, and it will never steer you wrong.

www.ingramcontent.com/pod-product-compliance
Lightning Source LLC
Chambersburg PA
CBHW060824050426
42453CB00008B/580